Inclusive Culture

Leading change across organisations and industries

Steve Butler

Rethink

First published in Great Britain in 2021
by Rethink Press (www.rethinkpress.com)

Contents

Introduction:
Diversity And Inclusion

'We believe that we have an extraordinary opportunity to press the reset button in our industry: to recruit, nurture and retain the first truly diverse generation of savings and investment professionals.'[1]

— The Diversity Project

I'm a white, middle-aged man, with nothing that would count as a disability. I'm not an obvious champion for diversity and inclusion. However, my journey to becoming chief executive of an investment and savings business with 150 staff tells its own story.

I attended state schools. Neither my parents nor my grandparents had a university education. A combination of this, my own lack of maturity and some dismal A-level results meant I never went to university either. Instead, I started my career at age eighteen as an office junior with an insurance company called AXA Equity and Law in Southampton and worked my way up.

The question I ask myself is this: would I have got where I am today if I had been Black, female or living with a disability... or perhaps all three?

There are some great examples in our industry of women, those from minority backgrounds and people from a much humbler economic background than mine who are in senior roles in the investment and savings sector. Some of their stories are featured in this book. Those people are few and far between though, and their road has been far more uncertain and arduous.

Importantly, an unknown – but certainly large – number of talented people have never even entered our industry, let alone fulfilled their potential in it, because of the roadblocks in their way. Those people have taken their talents elsewhere.

The investment and savings sector has a problem with minority groups. As an industry, it is nowhere near representative of the population as a whole, and the figures speak for themselves. In London, where the majority of fund managers are based, 18.5% of the population is Asian and 13.3% is Black.[2] Yet, in the fund-management industry, 10% of individuals identify as Asian and only 1% identify as Black.[3]

The proportion of female fund managers in the UK has hovered at around 10% over the past four years, and just 4% of money managed is overseen exclusively by women.[4] The pay gap between men and women in fund management is actually the second largest of any sector in the UK, with only investment banking registering worse figures.

Other specific comparators are hard to establish because of a lack of granular data (an issue I cover in this book). Look around you (or around your screen in your next Zoom or Teams meeting) and check, for instance, how many of your colleagues have a visible disability. Across the economy, slightly more than half of disabled people were in employment (53.2%) in 2019 compared with just over four out of five non-disabled people (81.8%),[5] and there's no reason to assume that the situation is any better in our own sector.

This situation needs to be addressed, and I want to play whatever part I can. Indeed, I have a responsibility to leverage my privilege to develop an inclusive culture – not only in my own business but also more widely in the workplace. It's not just a question of fairness, as important as that is to me. It's also a question of sound business practice.

In my own organisation of 150 people, we have worked hard over the last five years to embed an inclusive culture as a key element of our identity. That's resulted in an Investors in People silver accreditation, the Business in the Community Responsible Business Champion Age Award 2020, the Management Today NextGen Culture Award 2020 and the Reward Strategy Diversity and Inclusion Award 2019. Receiving these awards doesn't just feel great; it also influences the most important aspect of any business: the bottom line. Being recognised as an inclusive organisation attracts more talented people to work for us and new clients to hire us. The more cognitively, ethnically and socially diverse my teams are, the better they reflect the clients they serve, and the more effectively they can rise to the opportunities and challenges we are presented with.

I have seen the benefits of striving to create a diverse and inclusive culture in my company, even though we still have a way to go. I want to share what I have learned with other business managers. Moreover, as the contributors to this book make clear, addressing the lack of diversity and inclusion in our sector isn't down to those at the 'wrong end' of the in-built inequities. They aren't the ones responsible for a culture that has long made it hugely problematic for certain groups in society to achieve their full potential. They aren't the ones with the levers to effect change.

Just as racism in society isn't a Black problem but a white one, so too the systemic biases – often unconscious but still real – that make it harder for women and those from a range of minority groups to progress have to be resolved by those of us who are in a position to do so.

Why does this matter, and what's the solution?

Despite the educational, demographic and cultural shifts across society that we have witnessed in recent years, it is still far more difficult to rise to the top in the financial services sector if you do not come from a narrow band of the population: white males from wealthy backgrounds, privately educated, with a degree from a select group of universities.

Apart from the inequality of opportunity and unfairness this represents, it means that the sector is currently missing out on a huge talent pool, one that offers the life experiences and cognitive diversity that can tap more directly into the way other parts of the population live and think. That diversity of thinking can help businesses design new products and services that better meet the needs and ambitions of their clients. It also allows the industry as a whole to meet challenges in a way less hidebound by the groupthink that (arguably) led to the worst excesses of the last financial crisis.

That brings me on to another compelling argument for being a more diverse company: answering the question of where the next generation of talent is going to come from. In my 2019 book *Manage The Gap: Achieving success with intergenerational teams*,[6] I set out some of the many ways in which younger people coming into businesses or rising through the ranks see the world in a different way from previous generations.

5

They increasingly demand equality of opportunity for all – regardless of background, gender, ethnicity, disability or orientation. They expect to be allowed to strike a balance that allows them to have a family and personal life. They want the company they work for to embody ideals and social purposes that align with their own. If their employer can't deliver that, they may take their talents elsewhere. If the investment and savings sector fails to woo today's graduates, where will tomorrow's leaders come from?

Investors and clients (who are increasingly global) also expect the people who manage their money to have socially fair work practices in place, and to reflect themselves and the world they live in. The days when investors were primarily white men from a wealthy background, only comfortable with someone who echoed their own background to handle their business, are long gone.

The good news is that the investment and savings industry is doing something to ensure it keeps pace with the change and progress we are seeing in the rest of society, and that the sector is fit for purpose for the future. In early 2016, a group of leaders in the profession recognised that future success for their clients, members, employers and shareholders will require a far more inclusive culture and decided to take action to accelerate progress towards this. That led to establishing the Diversity Project, which has since gained huge support from across the sector and made big strides in raising awareness of the issues.

Where change needs to happen

In spite of some progress, there is still a long way to go for that awareness and support to translate into more people from diverse backgrounds entering and progressing in the sector. It is fundamental to embed inclusiveness into organisational culture if we want diversity and inclusion to be more than a window dressing. It is critical that this cultural change happens on many levels.

Firstly, it has to come from the top: business leaders must create the framework in their organisation for an inclusive culture to thrive. This book explains the things that leaders can do to make those changes in their organisation – including changing working practices that preclude certain groups and setting a personal example by openly welcoming and celebrating diversity.

It also has to be enabled and encouraged to happen at a grassroots level. That means empowering employees to take the ball and run with it, so inclusiveness becomes organic and takes on its own form: one that fits the organisation. Encouraging storytelling – getting people in the organisation to share their own lived experiences – is a key way of shaping that organic change. Storytelling not only gives everyone a voice but opens the door to empathy. Once everyone understands each other, they can make their own decisions about inclusivity, and that's a much more powerful tool than an edict from on high telling someone to be more inclusive.

The third level where change has to be driven is the industry itself: despite my efforts, I can't get the cognitive diversity I want in my business because the diverse group of people with the relevant experience I would dearly like to hire don't currently exist. We, as businesses, have to come together and talk about how we are going to recruit these people into the industry, and then bring them on. This is where the Diversity Project is making the difference.

This book draws heavily on the vision of the Diversity Project, which was set up to address the challenges listed above. It is grounded on the powerful personal stories and experiences of the people who are leading the project's workstreams. It is a 'what works' guide, built on the personal stories of leaders in the Diversity Project and members of my own team. Never underestimate the power of storytelling: we are all hardwired to resonate and respond to people's stories.

Scientists have tracked the neurochemical changes that take place in our brains while we listen to a story being told. Research by neuroeconomist Paul Zak has found that when we encounter a good story, our brain releases oxytocin, causing us to feel empathy; this can directly feed into motivating people to modify their behaviour. As Paul Zak explains:

'Oxytocin is produced when we are trusted or shown a kindness, and it motivates cooperation with others. It does this by enhancing the sense of empathy, our ability to experience others' emotions. Empathy is important for social creatures because it allows us to understand how others are likely to react to a situation, including those with whom we work.'[7]

Going beyond 'talking the talk'

Drawing on the collective knowledge and experiences of those steering the exceptional work of the Diversity Project, this book provides helpful guidelines for senior and middle managers who genuinely intend to make their businesses more inclusive. It suggests practical ways to create and foster a culture in which everyone in the company is on board with the mission of being truly diverse and inclusive.

Making sure that the business I manage is indeed reflective of society hasn't always been easy. It has meant radically adjusting the lens through which I see the world. At times, I have struggled to find the right words to use with staff from minority groups. I have had to find ways to encourage my teams to change the way they work and persuade people in my business that the effort is worth it. I have had to convince others that I am not simply paying lip service or virtue-signalling.

Walking the walk now means that when I recruit, I will consider an individual who doesn't have the qualifications and technical ability required for a role, or who doesn't slot in as a direct replacement – but who has the potential and will contribute most to their team. Often, I look for someone with a different perspective that will complement the others while challenging their and my thinking when necessary: that approach alone has led me to appoint (and subsequently promote) people I would never have considered before.

Recruiting a diverse and inclusive workforce is only one part of the equation. Retaining them and creating pathways for them to progress in your business is another. That presents another set of problems, which you'll read about in later chapters.

If there is one takeaway message that I can offer now, it is this: talk to your staff more; listen to them more; understand where they are coming from and the challenges they face away from work; discover and appreciate their ambitions. These people may be different from you, but because of that they can bring things to your business that you cannot. The world is changing, and the future belongs to those best able to adapt to their new environment. It's only by having open, meaningful conversations with the individuals you employ that you will make your company truly diverse and inclusive.

Three ways to make culture change stick

The Chartered Institute of Personnel and Development (CIPD) has excellent advice on how to introduce cultural change and, most importantly, how to make that change sustainable:[8]

1. Make regular, small changes in the organisation, rather than big grand changes which are more likely to make people concerned than to excite them.
2. Communicate the business need for change to the whole organisation, allowing time for individuals to consider the changes.
3. Use informal networks of employees to help implement a change of culture.

Definitions

For everyone to push in the right direction, it's helpful to use a common language. In this book, the key terms and distinctions have the following meanings.

Diversity and inclusion

The words diversity and inclusion are often used in the same breath, but they mean different things, both of which are important for organisations. According to the CIPD, diversity is about recognising the differences between people and 'acknowledging the benefit of having a range of perspectives'. Inclusion is about valuing those differences and creating a working environment where everyone 'feels that they belong without having to conform' and can 'perform to their full potential, no matter their background, identity or circumstances'.[9]

Rather more figuratively, Verna Myers has been credited with this neat distinction: 'Diversity is being invited to the party; inclusion is being asked to dance.'[10] In other words, opening the door to people from different walks of life and ways of thinking is a great first step, but it doesn't achieve anything unless those people are then enabled, encouraged and empowered to play a full role.

One of the issues discussed in this book is the number of people from different backgrounds who don't make it through to the upper echelons of a business. Look no further than the failure (after decades of trying) to get more women into top roles in the sector. There might be plenty of women working in the investment and savings sector, making it 'diverse', but the statistics mentioned earlier show that there is much more to do to make it a truly inclusive sector where women play a full part at every level.

Equality and equity

The Equality and Human Rights Commission describes equality as: 'Ensuring that every individual has an equal opportunity to make the most of their lives and talents.'[11] But 'equal' doesn't necessarily mean 'the same'.

There are many versions available of the equity v equality cartoon, all of which make the same point: treating everybody equally by giving them the same-sized box to stand on to see over the fence to watch a baseball game is not always enough. Sometimes you have to give some people a bigger box to make sure that everyone has the same opportunity – and that is equity.

For example, one of the issues raised in Chapter Four is that common recruitment interview techniques, which are designed to ensure everybody has an equal chance of doing their best, actually put those with certain neurodiversities at a major disadvantage. The same can apply to people with certain physical disabilities. If we want to make sure that someone who uses a wheelchair has an 'equal' chance of giving their best in an interview, we need to consider how they are going to get there, what different needs they might have when they arrive and whether they might need some adjustments to their working environment.

Intersectionality

Many groups are currently at a disadvantage when it comes to getting into, and progressing in, the invest-ment and savings sector, and the Diversity Project has set up workstreams dedicated to each of these.

Often, though, people have more than one hurdle to overcome: for instance, if you are a Black, gay, disabled woman. 'Intersectionality' considers all aspects of the disadvantages that certain groups experience, including how they overlap and compound each other.

Civil rights activist Kimberlé Williams Crenshaw makes clear that we need to consider these overlapping disadvantages: 'If we aren't intersectional, some of us, the most vulnerable, are going to fall through the cracks.'[12] This may seem challenging to many employers, but rather than looking at intersectionality as a complicating factor, my perspective is that, approached correctly, it can actually simplify matters. Later chapters make it plain that, if you take the position of making the workplace accessible to everyone, not least through inclusive recruitment policies and smart working practices, you open the door to all groups – and empower them to progress.

Organisational culture

'Organisational culture' has memorably been boiled down to 'the way we do things around here'[13]...and we all know what it's like to move company and find that the 'way they do things' is completely different from how they were done in the last place we worked.

Less prosaically, the CIPD defines organisational culture as the 'workplace norms, values and behaviours, traditions, perspectives and beliefs of individuals...shared characteristics among people within the same organisation.'[14] Organisational culture is driven from the top and then sustained by an unchallenging middle management. Even more importantly, organisational culture can be challenged – and changed.

The business benefits of diversity and inclusion

What is uppermost in your mind when you look to recruit a new member for your team or company? Are you looking for someone who has the same skills and background as the person they are replacing? Is it important that they come from a well-respected university? That they'll get on well with the rest of the team, and share a similar outlook to yours? That their 'face will fit'?

That's the safe route, and it's the traditional way that most of our industry has recruited. It's also why the industry lags so far behind similar sectors in the diversity of its workforce – especially at senior levels. Have you ever wondered if the safest route is actually the best way forward for the future of your business?

By taking the safe route, might you simply be recruiting someone who looks like you, acts like you, thinks like you and everyone else around them, and won't challenge the decisions you make? Could you really do with someone who might challenge you from time to time, question your time-honoured way of doing things, recognise opportunities that you would never have spotted, and come at things from a different direction?

The business argument for greater diversity and inclusion in the workplace is simply this: the more ways in which you can look at a problem, the better chance you have of solving it. Added to that is the fact that every business should reflect the clients and customers it serves if it really wants to understand and connect with them.

When I began in the industry, companies were run along broadly hierarchical lines: people stayed with an employer for years – often a lifetime. They patiently 'served their time' in a role before taking the place of the person above them, by which time they had been moulded into that person's way of working. The succession process was geared towards continuity, stability and safety: important factors in the finance business.

That might have worked then, but it would be a recipe for disaster today. Now we work largely in teams assembled for a specific purpose: light-footed groups that have to deal with regular changes of remit or even have to be rebuilt to deal with a new brief; teams that have to cope with frequent staff changes because no one stays in a job for long any more; teams that might draw on outside contractors for specific skills or to bolster capacity; teams that have to work across international boundaries; teams that need to empathise with highly diverse client bases.

In this new reality, the last thing you want is a group of people who look, think and act in a similar way. The 'clone approach' to recruitment – especially at a senior level – was one factor that increased the scale of the financial crisis, as Baroness Helena Morrissey DBE, chair of the Diversity Project, makes clear in an interview she kindly gave for this book. She has been at the forefront of persuading businesses to appoint more women to their boards: a task (as she candidly confesses) that is still a work-in-progress.

Helena Morrissey, Chair of the Diversity Project and Financier

Before the 2007/2008 crisis, it was hard to make a case on business grounds for having more women. There was talk about equal opportunities, diversity and inclusion networks and affinity groups, that sort of thing, but I always thought it made no sense to only have people from a very narrow educational background as well as the same gender, same geography, same social class, friends with each other. It's difficult for them to challenge each other. It's not human nature. Part of their identity is the group they associate with, and we're not programmed to undermine our own group.

I saw first-hand the trajectory of the Royal Bank of Scotland (RBS) going into the crash, because Newton Investment Management ran the pension fund and I ran all the fixed income part of that. Over the ten or so years prior to that, we had meetings in Edinburgh and saw their evolution from a group of mild, modest Scottish people to a situation where they were talking about installing helipads. After the last dinner we had with them, my colleagues and I came out of that room and said: 'My God....' It was quite plain to see how they had gone into this bubble where they could do no wrong.

In the aftermath of the financial crisis, people were talking about groupthink, and the regulators in their report cited lack of challenge in the downfall of RBS, as well as Fred Goodwin's dominating style. On the board were seventeen men and one woman, and most of the men were from Edinburgh. A few months before the crash they appointed an Englishman to the board, and this was trumpeted as a great example of diversity. They hung out together; many had been to the same school together.

I've always thought that if we have more diverse thinking around the table, we're more likely to come up with solutions to some of the problems that we face.

Helena Morrissey – the inspiration behind the Diversity Project – has long been an advocate of greater gender equality in the financial sector, and she is now leading the way on equality for other minority groups. The same argument applies: the greater the diversity of thinking, the better a team will perform. Critically, it acts as a defence against the groupthink that has bedevilled our sector and made those who practise it vulnerable.

In *Manage The Gap*,[15] I focused on the need for businesses to blend abilities and backgrounds to succeed. Drawing on my personal experience of mountaineering in the Himalayas, I've seen first-hand how the only way to get a group up (and down) a mountain safely is to select everyone for their role, and have them focus on what they do best. That team could include the motivational leader, who instinctively knows how to get each individual to keep going at difficult times; the orienteer, who is skilled with map and compass; the person whose rope expertise you can truly count on when you hit a crevasse; the medic in the party; and the cooks and porters. Teams in the workplace are no different. You want to able to pick a side that has a blend of abilities to achieve your goals. Diversity in a team is a strength, not a weakness. Eleven orienteers on a mountain climb might look good on paper but would be totally unbalanced.

As I write in *Manage The Gap*, 'A fusion of different ways of thinking and varying life experiences enriches the workplace, and that's been borne out by countless surveys and endorsements.'[16] One of those endorsements comes from William S Demchak, Chair, President and CEO of PNC Financial Services: 'A diverse and multigenerational workforce better positions PNC to understand and provide for our customers' evolving preferences.'

In the pages that follow, I look at gender and age among other kinds of diversity – including ethnicity, neurodiversity and economic background – but the overarching message is the same: the more diverse your workforce, the richer the pool of talent you can call on to take your business forwards. As the CIPD states in its resource *Diversity and Inclusion in the Workplace*:

> 'Everyone stands to benefit when we embrace and value the diversity of thoughts, ideas and ways of working that people from different backgrounds, experiences and identities bring to an organisation. So organisations must ensure their people-management approaches do not put any group at a disadvantage.'[17]

I'll leave the final words of this chapter to Jane Welsh, one of the founders of the Diversity Project who I interviewed while writing this book:

> 'What we're pushing for is culture change if we're to create more inclusive organisations. The end benefit to companies is cognitive diversity within the business: there are lots of ways to define it, but basically, it's people

who think differently...perhaps the big picture, perhaps the small detail. The evidence suggests that if you have a group of people who all think alike, even if they are very smart, they are going to miss things.

'If you have a group of people who look at the world differently, and if people listen to those different viewpoints, which is always the challenge, there's a chance that they might pick up some of those risks or opportunities.'

ONE

Gender

'Young women coming in – and there aren't enough of them – don't feel confident that they will see it through, or they get fed up and leave to do something else.'

— Baroness Helena Morrissey DBE,
  Chair of the Diversity Project[18]

Challenges and issues

Lack of gender equality is still an issue in many parts of the UK economy, but especially in the investment and savings industry. Currently, gender pay gaps in asset management are the second largest of any UK sector: only 10% of fund managers are female and just 4% of money managed in the UK is headed up exclusively by women.[19]

The problem could be one of recruitment, development or an inability of firms to accommodate career breaks, or perhaps a combination of all three. Staff turnover in the industry is relatively slow, so there are fewer opportunities for advancement, but that alone does not explain it.

Perhaps surprisingly, getting into the sector in the first place can be more difficult today than it was twenty years ago, as Diversity Project co-founder Jane Welsh recounts:

Jane Walsh, Co-founder, Diversity Project

When we started out in our careers, although the industry was tiny compared to today, there was a higher proportion of senior women around than there is now. We wondered why that might be, and this was one of the triggers for a small group of us setting up the Diversity Project.

That observation led to a second observation: if we started out today, would we even get a job in the industry? Both because of the way that big firms recruit at graduate level, focusing on particular universities and people with particular subject backgrounds, and because of self-selection by students.

There is a perception that, unless you're studying maths, finance or economics, you wouldn't consider a career in this industry. And unless your mum or dad, uncle or aunt, worked in this industry, you wouldn't even know about it.

The chronic lack of women in the most senior roles is not confined to the investment and savings sector. According to gender diversity business The Pipeline, 15% of companies in the FTSE 350 have no female executives at all, and just fourteen of those companies are led by women.[20]

By having such a low ratio of senior women in key roles, our industry is missing out on profitability as well as equality. The Pipeline's 2020 report says that London-listed companies with no women on their executive committees have a net profit of 1.5%, while those with more than one in three women at that level have recorded an average net profit margin of 15.2%.[21] Having a better gender ratio may not be the only factor in this bigger profit, but those companies are probably more forward-thinking – and cognitive diversity is part of forward-thinking.

Lived experiences

Once women get into the industry there can be further roadblocks to encounter, as Claire Black, one of the leaders of the Diversity Project's Working Families workstream, explains. Her story illustrates the multiple challenges faced by women who want to progress in their careers while raising a family.

Claire Black, Working Families Workstream Leader

For me, the problems of combining work and raising a family started even before my first child arrived eight years ago: I had fertility treatment, and I didn't receive the support from my employer I thought I would have. In fact, I was told that, because it was 'elective surgery', I would get five additional days' leave and that was it – regardless of how many attempts I would need. All of which made a highly stressful situation even more difficult, and stress is the last thing you need at that point in your life.

After that, I encountered the pressures that most women face. You return from maternity and there's an expectation that you're just going to jump back into your job 100%. It doesn't work like that. As well as having to get back up to speed, part of your brain is taken up with babies. The pressure of trying to get everything done, then rushing off to pick up your child, is enormous. In addition, of course, taking maternity leave impacts upon your career progression: there is this assumption that you are no longer so committed to your role and your career.

I came back to work four days a week because it was all I could possibly do: I was exhausted. However, that was made more complicated because during my pregnancy my marriage broke down and I became a single parent. I quickly had to go back to five days because I couldn't financially support myself on a

20% pay cut. So, coming back there was an extra pressure that I had to do this: it was my job keeping the roof over our heads.

My line manager was aware of my situation during my maternity leave, but I didn't have any one-to-one follow-up support to check on how it was working for me. I was still breastfeeding, so I was expressing at work and had to fit that around meetings. This was uncomfortable as well as difficult. I know companies do accommodate that and have a lactation room; but if you're made to feel guilty, or you don't have that window to go and do that when you need to, that makes it difficult.

All this is going on while you want to keep performing for your company. I felt this pressure that I was still expected to do my job – and exactly how I had done it when I left. And I am a high-performing individual, focused on my career.

For me it was really important to take my son to school one day a week so I would have that touchpoint with his teachers, so I had to apply for flexible working. Even then, it was reviewed every three months. At one point it was taken away from me for a year because it was felt that, being a line manager myself, I had to be visible to my team – even though I had people in my office who had line managers in the US.

Having support internally at this critical time would have made a huge difference to me.

But there was no real conversation about my role changing in any way. All that said, this was eight years ago and, certainly in my case, the people and support has changed since then. I've had an extremely difficult time this year – and my line manager has been very supportive.

As Claire Black says, individual companies are making progress, but it isn't uniform. If an employer gains a reputation for having an unsympathetic approach to women who are combining a career and a family, it will inevitably deter many women from joining them or staying with them for longer.

Helena Morrissey has been tackling the issue of gender equality in the sector for many years, and has become a role model for women who have the ambition to achieve their full potential. Here is her take.

Helena Morrissey, Chair

When I joined my first investment company back in 1987, the month of the Crash, they sent me out straight from a graduate programme to New York. My experiences there were pretty favourable: there were four people around the office, two men who ran the money and two women who ran the business, and the women seemed to call the shots – to my naive eyes, anyway! They were certainly very highly regarded and very much in control of their own destiny. In hindsight, they were also great role models for me, but what I didn't appreciate at the time was how unusual it was to have that gender balance.

I came back to London after two years to find myself the only woman in the team and immediately recognised that the situation in New York had been quite anomalous. I then got married and, within a year, had my first child. That exposed me rather abruptly to gender issues within the industry. This was the era when people talked openly in the office about going to lap-dancing clubs with clients. There was a lot of banter, and I'd wince and try to hide away.

When I came back from maternity leave and had my first conversation with my boss, I was eligible for my first promotion from graduate trainee to manager. I didn't get it, while all my male peers did. I asked what I was doing wrong and was told: 'Your performance is great – but there's some doubt about your commitment because of you having a baby.'

I'd only taken five months off. I'd kept up with developments, having investment papers dropped through my letterbox every week. I wasn't showing any sign of being less committed. I remember challenging him, and being told that his boss – also obviously a man – was 'quite old fashioned' about these things.

It was a rude awakening. Until then, probably naively, I'd never thought starting a family could have any impact on my career. I realised that I had to make a decision: put up, shut up or move on.

I didn't move immediately because I had a small child and a lot of things going on, but I started looking around and was headhunted about a year later to join Newton Investment Management, which was quite different...not least because my boss was a woman.

The founder, Stewart Newton, interviewed me and told me that they had a special maternity policy that provided about six months' full pay and then helped you to return to work. They were very proactive about being family friendly, and also welcomed diversity of thought. After I was appointed, Stewart mentored me, and I remember him saying: 'Don't ever hide the fact that you're a mother. Or be embarrassed about any of the things you need to do around that. That's part of your perspective. It's what brings you to this firm and what makes you different.'

He had built the whole firm around this philosophy that diversity of thought (although he called it 'multiple perspectives', as no one then was using the word 'diversity') would achieve the best investment results. In that, he was well ahead of his time.

I should add that my first company did then have two powerful women in the London office. The rest of the firm was very hierarchical, traditional, silver-trolleyed, butlers – stuff they would wince at now – but at the other end there was this little club of women that was mutually supportive. In contrast, Newton had a culture of diversity running through it like the words in a stick of rock, although I didn't realise quite how unusual that was at the time.

We took pride in being something of a motley crew and loved gathering people who had an interesting perspective. Everybody had a quirk. That said, everyone was polished enough and had a real passion for what they did. Our strapline then was 'no one has a monopoly on great ideas'. The firm had a boutique feel, and clients seemed to like having characterful people's approach to money.

Looking back, the culture was key. Having failed at the first hurdle in my first job, I became CEO at age thirty-five with five children, seven years after joining and that was all down to the cultural differences. It was very meritocratic, and if you wanted responsibility, you'd be given it. But even when I became chief executive, I felt I had to earn that job: I had the title but not the mandate, so I never did anything around diversity or gender for several years.

Around 2005, I was asked to join the board of the Investment Association as their first female director – and that was an eye-opener. I'd be chatting to the other board members and realise that they'd gone to prep school together forty years before! There was no desire to change anything within the industry. Everybody was quite comfortable with their lot. Within my own firm, I discussed starting a women's development network – I became the co-chair of Mellon International, Newton's parent company, so I used that as a platform to get something going inside the firm. I focused on the women in Newton and across the rest of Mellon in EMEA, and we ran lots of events and workshops around career development.

But my efforts weren't entirely successful. It tended to be women talking to women about women's issues. Men were still very much a minority. We lacked clear-cut measurable targets, so there was no way of knowing if we were getting anywhere.

And then came the financial crisis, so no one could exactly claim things were perfect. That's when I started to talk to women outside the industry: I got a group together of about forty women and we agreed that we were making very little progress in senior roles and on boards. Most of the women were sceptical about the progress possible. They certainly wanted it to happen, but they felt worn down by their experiences. The most typical reaction was, 'We won't be able to change anything.'

The genesis of the 30% Club is well documented. I was invited to speak on diversity and inclusion at a lunch – there was a mix of men and women from different sectors – and we discussed how difficult it was to make much progress beyond around 10% women at senior levels. That's when I had a lightbulb moment: I came away thinking it doesn't make any sense. We've got ready, able and willing women feeling frustrated with the situation, and companies that want them to progress. *What are we doing wrong?*

I started reading widely around organisational behaviours and how you achieve change. That's when I read about Deutsche Telekom trying to get 30% women on all levels – and for business reasons: to get the best talent, the best thinking. And I realised that in groups where women make up one-third, you feel part of the group. Fewer than that and you can feel a bit token. That's where the 30% target came from.

Despite making some progress over the last five years, there is still so much more to do – which is why we 'relaunched' in July 2020 with new targets, which include a halving of the industry's gender pay gaps and a 30% female fund manager target by 2030. Citywire has done an Alpha Female report for four years and their data shows we've crept up from 10.2% fund managers around the world to 10.8% in that time – so there's a long way to go.

Compared with the time when I joined the industry, I think it's probably more off-putting for women now joining because we were blissfully ignorant. When I was interviewed on the 'milk round', men and women were applying, and interviews were with a man-and-woman panel. Diana Noble, who interviewed me, had a big influence on me.

I do think that behaviours generally are – I wouldn't say perfect – but more subtle now around the issues that women face. We might not get the banter I had to put up with, but sometimes it's quite insidious. Women are led to believe they will be quite welcome, and that's true in many firms but sometimes poor behaviours – patronising talk or simply not being managed properly – still get in the way. I now see great commitment to resolve these issues though and that's exciting.

When I joined the industry, it felt the only way to get on was by being an 'honorary man', and that takes away from the whole point about diversity. Young women coming in – and there aren't enough of them – should feel confident that people are much more aware of this and the need to value people for what they bring to the table. Fund management is a fabulous career for anyone who wants to be measured on results. I know that ultimately enabled me to succeed; it wasn't about hours worked at the same desk, it was about making the right judgements.

Now we have a sense of urgency about it – no stone unturned, every stage of the career, every aspect of the problem. I think the investment industry generally has been slow on diversity and inclusion, and a little bit arrogant – which is ironic when they themselves pressure companies on these issues. The pandemic has created a crossroads moment; many women have struggled both in our industry and of course more broadly in society as we've borne the brunt of childcare and other domestic duties, but we've also been able to demonstrate that we can all work productively from home. It's given a glimpse into how things could be more modern, more genuinely family friendly.

Firms can choose to make a conscious decision to ensure that women don't slide backwards. Ideally, we'll end up in a position where men as well as women can have real work-life balance and that will enable more women to take advantage of career opportunities. We need to make a conscious decision to create that different working environment now.

Towards the end of 2020, as part of a company-wide series of online panel discussions on diversity and inclusion, three of my female colleagues provided their insights into experiences of gender inequality. They each come from different age groups and their experiences make clear that, although things have improved for women in our industry in the last thirty years, they are still a long way from being acceptable.

Jane Kelly, Employee Benefit Consultant

I started work in the 1980s with an insurance company in Manchester, and it was definitely a very unequal environment…but it's only by looking back that I now see that, and that it should have been challenged.

All of the managerial and sales roles were held by men; the office staff were female. Every Friday at midday, all the men would go down to the pub while we carried on working, and eventually we'd be invited to join them. We didn't think there was anything wrong with that…it's just the way it was.

When we did appoint a female broker, which was quite unusual at the time, she was treated really badly by the other consultants. She wasn't included in anything. There would be days out…rugby matches, golf, football, days at the pub…things that excluded her. And they made it quite obvious that they were excluding her.

Even we actually wondered why she *was* doing that job. Now I look back, I think it was horrible. We should have supported her more. If it was now, I would challenge it without any doubt, but I came from a background where that happened in the home. Back then, it didn't seem an issue.

I was bullied and treated very unfairly by my manager when I was expecting my first child. It was 1989 and as soon as I notified him, he made it very clear that *his* wife wouldn't dream of going back to work after having a baby: it was terrible to leave a child at home and I should be ashamed of myself.

When I did go back – not least because I needed to financially – he put a load of work on me, challenged everything I did, questioned my performance. Despite the fact that we were hitting every target, he put me under so much pressure. I was going into work when I wasn't well, simply because I knew he would use that as another thing to pressure me with.

That has had a big effect on me, and changed the way I expect to be treated in the workplace. I haven't pushed myself forward. I've felt I've always had to justify myself more than a man.

I've managed to turn things around, have since had a good career. The turning point is when you start to work for people who allow you to grow and have some good role models.

Paraplanner

I started in the workplace in the mid-1990s as part of a compliance training unit that eventually totalled around 200 people. These were largely graduates with a broad mix of males and females, although some came from different backgrounds.

My first experience of gender inequality was after my first son was born in 2003. I went back to work part time, and that was frowned upon. They wanted me to be full time, so I had to really push to do a three-day week. In addition, I wasn't allowed back to my previous role although there was no reason why I couldn't do it. I stayed in that job for a year. Over that time, I would be sitting at the nursery gates at 7.30 in the morning waiting to drop him off and then hoping I could make it back before it shut at 6.30. My mum-in-law helped one day a week with childcare even though she lived an hour and a half away and had to come over the night before. On one occasion my son was ill and I was told to make my mum-in-law stay an extra day to look after him so that I could work. Like my peers, I carried on taking exams, but I was categorically told that, because I was part time, I'd only be paid a bonus pro rata, even though it wasn't a pro-rata qualification.

I left that job after a year to be closer to my family, but there weren't any jobs at the time that would fit in with what I needed to do, so I decided I would have to leave the industry and actually started to train as a childminder. Then just one comment to a friend changed everything. I said that if her firm ever wanted a part-time paraplanner working from home, please think of me. Within two weeks I had a job created for me, and that changed my career path. I was unfortunately made redundant after five years.

I have had two further jobs since. Both came about through submitting CVs to agencies that, although keen, weren't overly optimistic that I would find a part-time paraplanner role. There was certainly nothing to apply for on that basis. However, through the agencies sending out my CV on both occasions, companies needing some extra support then approached me and roles were created for me.

One other occasion springs to mind where I was basically told I couldn't progress in my career because I was part time. Since then I have been promoted to a part-time team leader and now manager.

Employee Communications Consultant

When I joined the industry, I was blissfully unaware of inequality for a long time. On my university accountancy course, there was a balance. So too the graduate intake, although looking back, most managers were men.

What I have come to be particularly aware of are the unconscious biases and unconscious shortcuts that still play out. They aren't malicious and – by their very nature – we often don't notice what's happening. For example, when I joined the graduate scheme I met my best friend, and we both met our fiancées there. This was seven years ago and at that time we were all very much on a level playing field in terms of qualifications and salary. Last year, my partner earned double what I earned. My friend's partner earns more than double her salary.

There are loads of reasons that drive that pay divide, but one contributory factor, as my partner will tell you, is that he has experienced unconscious shortcuts in his career. For instance, a big part of the graduate scheme was networking, and it was a lot easier for him to network with the level above. If I was having a one-to-one with a male leader, I was very conscious of not being flirty, and actively avoided those one-on-one conversations. In our induction we were told: 'Boys, don't wear one of Dad's suits; girls, don't wear short skirts.'

The senior levels were male-dominated, and my partner could find common ground easier than I could. He could talk about cricket or red wine. I struggled to have conversations with those older men, because I didn't know what to talk about unless it was about work. That held me back in my networking, and those unconscious shortcuts still exist in the workplace.

That isn't to say that men shouldn't have personal rapport. Just be aware of how it might affect your decision-making. Managers need to be aware of the unconscious shortcuts they can give colleagues. Women also must not be afraid – or be made to feel afraid – of having conversations about their career or pay, because many do have a natural reluctance to do that. And managers must encourage women to have those conversations. Women should also be involved when it comes to designing a benefits structure that works for all of the staff and take on board female health, motherhood, fertility issues – which males might not naturally think of.

Leading change to gender equality

One of the challenges in my own company is that we have grown rapidly over the last few years as we acquired regionally based businesses. Some of those companies have far more 'traditional' cultures, management techniques and working practices than the one I have been running since 2015. Another challenge is that although the company has a London base, it's a fairly decentralised organisation, which can make it more difficult to standardise approaches across the business. This has proven to be an ideal template for testing and embedding new working practices across a company: if we can make it work, anyone can. By sharing that experience, I aim to help you, as a manager, change your organisation's culture to promote gender equality.

As part of our commitment to creating a balanced workforce, we are making the following changes:

- Driving better gender balance, diversity and inclusion at all levels in the organisation

- Establishing operational committees in key areas of the business, providing the opportunity for broader involvement and diversity in the management structure

- Developing female talent in the organisation through training and mentoring

- Supporting and encouraging greater female participation in meetings, projects and teams

- Seeking new strong female talent to join the business

- Encouraging a better work/life balance and flexible working for all employees to support families and retain talent

- Increasing diversity and inclusion content in induction training and all aspects of our employee life cycle

- Being aware of unconscious bias and promoting inclusive leadership through our development at all levels

Setting out commitments is one thing but achieving them is another. One of the first challenges I addressed was the under-representation of female employees in the management structure. As part of the commitment to diversity and inclusion in general, I replaced the existing executive committee of eight senior male managers with seven operational committees that included representatives from across the business. This led to more diverse, multigenerational teams contributing to the leadership and business strategy, and participation from women at management-level operational committee meetings increased from 0% to 38%.

Team meetings are rather different too. They begin with a 'sign-in' where each attendee takes a minute or two to update the others on what's happening in their life, particularly their personal development and wellbeing. Although there was some hesitance at first, everyone has fully embraced the approach, not least because it signals that our priority as a business is the welfare of our people. Starting the meeting with a personal reflection breaks down reserve and sets the tone for the meeting; then, when you reach the business section, people are much more transparent and responsive, and the meeting is far more productive. It also creates better understanding of what other pressures people in the team are dealing with in their lives. This can reduce disagreements and tensions, heading potential rifts off at the pass. Knowing what issues they are facing also gives you insights into how to manage individuals in that team. It has improved team communication and increased openness and understanding. Critically, it has broken down the macho approach that's so common in finance businesses, where sales and profit are the beginning, middle and end of meetings.

Women taking part in the new style of management meetings say that having their voices heard and valued has opened a door. Many have fed back to me that being involved in these meetings has increased their confidence, and participating in decision-making has broadened their horizons.

Personal objectives for managers

Another powerful tool for driving greater gender equality in the business is our bonus structure. We recalibrated this so that achieving diversity and inclusion objectives represents 30% of the potential bonus for senior managers: a potent incentive!

Examples of these objectives include:

- Having a one-to-one meeting with every female employee benefits consultant in the division to discuss their medium-term career ambitions and implement a learning and development plan for realising those ambitions

- Promoting an inclusive culture across the Employee Benefit Division through professional development, team-building activities and communication, and industry outreach

Reverse mentoring

In common with many other companies, we have embraced reverse mentoring: when the mentee is the older or more senior person in the pair, and the mentor is the younger or more junior person. Although we didn't introduce reverse mentoring solely to encourage gender equality, it has played a key role in achieving just that – motivating a significant number of women to progress their careers with us.

In reverse mentoring, the payoff for the mentee is that they gain insight into a different generation or culture and find out more about practices and ideas from someone outside their typical circle. Given the current situation in our industry, women are more likely to be the mentor in this pairing. That has allowed senior male staff to gain insights into the lives, challenges, pressures and ambitions of younger women in the business.

Senior managers can learn from a female mentor about things that their customers might also be experiencing, feeling, believing or liking. In the mentor role, women can gain visibility with the senior management team, displaying the talent that the company is developing as they look to the future.

Reverse mentoring can be challenging, and some of the first few meetings can be uncomfortable or even awkward. The senior manager may struggle with taking advice from someone who is in a more junior role in the organisation; a more junior employee may not feel comfortable with being transparent about their concerns and priorities or with challenging the thinking of someone who could hinder their career. The most important factor that will shape these meetings in the positive manner intended is mutual respect.

The Diversity Project approach

Working towards gender equality in the investment and savings sector has always been a major focus for the Diversity Project; but, in the words of the workstream leaders: 'To date efforts around gender have been greater than the results. A new approach is needed, with greater intensity and more targeted interventions.'[22] In 2020 this recognition led to a 'reboot' of the Gender Equality workstream's targets: 30% female fund managers and a halving of the investment industry's gender pay gaps by 2030.

Helena Morrissey, Chair of the Diversity Project and Founder of the 30% Club, elaborates:

'All the evidence suggests we continue to make painfully slow progress towards encouraging more women into fund management and to build their careers in our industry. At the same time, a sense of fatigue has set in around the topic of gender diversity. Yet the arguments for having more women run money, manage people, lead client relationships and contribute to our industry's culture and future are stronger than ever.

'We've analysed the obstacles and devised a new intensive, wide-ranging set of initiatives to address them and create new enablers for women to progress. And we've decided to set ambitious goals to hold our collective feet to the fire and actually deliver the progress needed.'[23]

The new gender workstream is being led by Helena Morrissey herself, and six subgroups are already working on approaches related to the following aspects:

- Line manager attitudes and lack of people-management training

- Industry culture, job design and career mapping

- Mentoring and sponsorship opportunities

- Industry reputation and role models

- Joining up employee records before and after a career break to maintain continuity

- Metrics that help firms understand their own problem areas

A subgroup of the Diversity Project's advisory council chaired by Stephen Welton is working on the leadership aspects of the issue. Describing their approach, Stephen says: 'On an individual level, key to this is challenging internal biases and "unlearning" many of the unconscious assumptions that perpetuate the gender inequality that still exists today.'[24]

To achieve ambitions for gender equality, the Diversity Project is focusing on smart working, returners and working families. It is also partnering with experts including City Hive,[25] Moving Ahead,[26] Women Returners,[27] upReach[28] and Timewise[29]. The project hopes to build on the progress made towards flexible working during the Covid-19 crisis, as flexibility is key to persuading more women to enter the sector and stay in it. For more on this, read Chapter Eight: Build Back Better.

The Diversity Project makes the following practical suggestions for improving gender equality:

- Start by tracking your diversity data. Don't just look at numbers of employees but also consider roles, retention and progression. What do the numbers tell you about recruitment, turnover, the distribution of performance ratings and the gender pay gap?

- Make sure your recruitment processes aren't holding women back. For example, does your website portray a diverse workforce, and are your job descriptions gender-neutral?

- Ensure all job postings emphasise smart working options. Smart working is a broad term for a variety of work patterns that do not fit into the traditional 9am to 5pm, five days a week. Examples include flexitime and part-time working.

- Don't ask about a candidate's previous salary. Why perpetuate any gender pay gap that might exist?

- Try to hire in clusters. That way, it's much easier to hire diverse talent. For example, when hiring graduates, recruit them together as part of a wider strategy at times in the academic year when the widest possible talent pool is available. This gives you more choice than if you recruited individual graduates as and when you need to fill a role.

- Insist on diverse shortlists and a balance of men and women on the interview panels.

- Use structured interview processes and cognitive tests. This will ensure you collect objective and comparable data on candidates.

- Consider a returnship programme to attract and support women who have taken an extended career break.

- Appoint people who will add the most to the team through complementary skills and perspectives, while avoiding tokenism.

- Ensure that succession and talent-management processes consider women in the broader context of diversity.

- Support mentoring and sponsorship for women.

- Provide extra support around career breaks. Mentoring before, during and after maternity leave, for example, can help women continue with their career progression. Revisit your smart working policies and practices to make sure they cover career breaks.

- If you have a gender pay gap, have a plan for closing it, starting by encouraging transparency about salaries.

- Encourage the business leaders to be role models.

- At meetings, techniques like turn-taking, active listening and requiring unanimity can ensure that women feel listened to and that the team benefits from diverse viewpoints. This is even more important on video or conference calls.

- Embed smart working throughout the business and encourage everyone to be as effective as they can be: it's OK for different people in a team to work in different ways, because we all need different things at different stages of our career.[30]

The CIPD perspective

The CIPD has the following additional pointers for organisations focusing on gender equality:[31]

- Make sure managers who are responsible for hiring are aware of any assumptions and biases they have that may influence the recruitment process.

- Create a wider culture of inclusion in the business, where difference is valued. The influence of that inclusive culture will lead to a fair and robust recruitment process.

Five things to do

1. Use senior management to engage and develop a medium-term career plan for all women, and develop a learning and development plan for each to help them realise those ambitions.

2. Restructure the business or implement new cross-business project teams to enable a broader group of people to take part in leadership and strategy decisions.

3. Set up reverse mentoring for senior male managers or middle managers to expose them to a different perspective and remove any blind spots in their management approach. Reverse mentoring also gives younger women in the business a profile with senior management.

4. Manage the male banter and male conversation in management and project meetings, giving everyone the opportunity to contribute. Using a sign-in process removes barriers or stereotyping in a meeting.

5. Review your recruitment process to ensure all job postings emphasise smart working options. Don't ask about previous salary, and insist on diverse shortlists and diverse interview panels. Use structured interview processes and cognitive tests to give you objective and comparable data on candidates.

TWO

Ethnicity

'If everyone joins hands and comes alongside us, then we can change the system and we can improve ourselves. All of us. Every one of us. We're all part of the problem or part of the solution. There's no more safe middle ground. And when you do nothing, you're part of the problem.'

— Dawid Konotey-Ahulu, Business Founder[32]

The challenges and issues

The UK is the world's second largest savings market after the United States, and our industry employs 100,000 people. Despite its size, it does not represent the wider population in terms of ethnicity. Ethnic minorities comprise 14% of the UK population, with 7.5% identifying as Asian and 3.3% as Black.[33] In London, where the majority of fund managers are based, 18.5% of the population is Asian and 13.3% is Black.[34] Yet, within fund management, 10% of individuals identify as Asian and just 1% identify as Black.[35]

Recent research by the *Financial Times* identifies a more troubling trend in the US financial services industry: that the proportion of Black employees in senior roles has fallen over the last ten years.[36] This is despite the fact that Black employees represent the largest proportion of ethnic minorities and there have been widespread initiatives designed to improve racial diversity.

The statistics highlight the urgency to address the issue for Black employees, but the real question is why the disparity? Speak to those directly affected and you'll be told there is no one simple answer and no 'magic bullet'. Some of the problems are deep rooted and societal. Some are simply not recognised as 'problems' by the people who are in a position to make a difference.

Members of the Diversity Project's Ethnicity workstream interviewed for this book apply the metaphor of 'kinks in the hose' when you're trying to water the garden. You straighten the piece of hose that's closest to you, but still no water flows. That's because there are more kinks further back. Get rid of those, and you'll find even more. You need to go right back to the tap, unkinking the hose at each point to get the water flowing.

In the context of ethnicity, you might well introduce diversity and inclusion practices in the workplace (removing one kink), and they may be adopted with enthusiasm; but social investment and access to education in our society (kinks further back in the hose) are critical if those practices are to be effective. Unless you get those kinks straightened, young people will never get the qualifications they need to reach the application stage or feel they could even belong in the investment and savings sector. Quite reasonably, businesses will argue that they can only remove the kinks that are closest to them, but there are ways in which companies and individuals can play a part in changing the bigger picture.

One factor complicating this issue is that not all ethnic minorities struggle equally to make their mark. Some (but not all) groups fare significantly better than others. This has led to the Diversity Project's Ethnicity workstream focusing much of its attention on Black rather than Asian communities.

As the Diversity Project has discovered, the issues are varied and complex when considering how to make progress across all the ethnic-minority groups. Therefore, for the purpose of this book, I have mirrored the approach taken by the Diversity Project and focused on Black employees. The project launched a #TalkAboutBlack initiative in June 2020, bringing together their thinking so far and reaching out to a much wider audience than ever before in the industry. In reality, ethnicity is worthy of a book in its own right.

The bigger picture

The Black Lives Matter campaign powerfully made the case that racism – in the UK as well as the US – is systemic, and that only root-and-branch shifts in culture, attitudes, public policies and education, combined with a better understanding of history, will lead to meaningful long-term change.

Gavin Lewis, a managing director and one of the leaders of the Diversity Project's Ethnicity workstream, gives his view on how much long-standing, underlying attitudes increase the challenge that Black people face when trying to reach their full potential in British society:

Gavin Lewis, Ethnicity Workstream Leader

Part of the problem can be tracked back to cultural differences – some of which are deeply rooted in history. In Britain, any conversation about slavery, and the part that Britain played in the slave trade, has routinely been quickly closed down. Because it happened 200 years ago, it isn't supposed to have any bearing on where we are now, so why do we even talk about it?

Thankfully, one of the positives that has come out of the tragic death of George Floyd, and the subsequent leap in public awareness of the Black Lives Matter campaign, has been that slavery and its continuing grip on the relationship between Black people and the rest of society has opened up the discussion – even if the two sides of the debate seem even more divided than before. The toppling of one statue of a slave trader in Bristol has led to similar actions right around the world.

My perspective? I know it's a thorny subject; however, all of this does have a bearing because you're talking about 400 years of displacement of a people, placing them in a situation where they are powerless, economically enslaved – and I don't think that situation has changed.

After migrants arrived in the UK, we still didn't have enough aspiration – not least because we'd been made to feel that it wasn't our place to aspire. And so, when Black people have got into our industry, they feel that they have little or no chance of getting up the ladder...not helped by the fact that there aren't any Black role models above them. It's a vicious circle: we don't aspire to reach the top, and the people who are at the top think you should be happy with what you've got.

My perspective

As I made clear at the start of this book, I'm white. In that case, what has all this got to do with me?

Like everyone reading this book, I suspect, I was deeply upset by the death of George Floyd. I also believed – rather naively – that there was little I could do. But I was wrong. As has since been eloquently expressed by many people, racism is not a Black person's problem; it's a white person's problem. Unless white people deal with it, it won't go away.

Since then, I have been on a journey of self-education and reflection that has fundamentally changed how I see the world. Back in May 2020, before George Floyd's death, I thought that:

- Because I treated everyone the same, I did not have racist views

- Because the investment and savings industry is a professional, regulated industry and I had a Black friend doing well in his career, the industry was not institutionally racist

- Because I lived in multicultural London and society worked OK, society was not structurally racist

I now understand – indeed, I am ashamed to say – that those views, in themselves, are not only incorrect and unquestioning but also racist. They represent part of the problem that is preventing change.

When I discussed this with my father, he asked what had happened to change my views so significantly. I reflected on this and identified the following things:

1. Firstly, the death of George Floyd and the Black Lives Matter campaign made me sit up and think... *really* think... about the lives of Black people, not just in the US but here in the UK.

2. Importantly, someone in my company was brave enough to ask: 'What does our business think about this?'

3. With my wife and daughter, I attended a small Black Lives Matter protest on Kew Green, where a few hundred people, socially distanced, knelt for ten minutes at the side of the road. I felt moved by the power of this demonstration.

4. I spoke for two hours with my only Black friend in the asset-management industry. We discussed all his experiences and the challenges he encountered in developing his career – and he opened up in a way he never had before.

5. I watched various webinars – including those shared by the Diversity Project – and I read an excellent book by Reni Eddo-Lodge called *Why I'm No Longer Talking to White People About Race*.[37]

6. I listened to the personal stories of people like Gavin Lewis, which led me to realise just how many hurdles Black people still have to overcome.

I now believe there is plenty I can do, and pretending there isn't a problem is not an option. As one contributor says later in this book, if you're not part of the solution then you're part of the problem; so, along with many other white people in the industry, I am trying to find ways to be part of the solution. Being an active member of the Diversity Project was a first and important step. The initiatives I have introduced into my company as a result are a second step, although these are still a work-in-progress. The third step is sharing what I have learned in this book.

Lived experiences

A point that Gavin Lewis and others repeatedly make is that to fully understand where Black employees are coming from, all employees need to listen to their perspective.

The #TalkAboutBlack initiative that began in 2020 electrified those fighting for diversity and inclusion in our industry. It brought together the industry to look with a sharper focus at the under-representation of Black people in the sector and led to a pipeline of actions that could make a long-term difference.

Critically, it opened up channels of communication between Black people working in the industry and those of us who want to 'be part of the solution' but don't quite know how. The mere act of listening to the voices of Black people, hearing their personal stories, understanding the barriers that they face, and which are not part of our lived experiences... all this can help build bridges.

In June 2020, the Diversity Project initiative #TalkAboutBlack hosted a panel discussion on racial injustice and what to do about it. Here are some of the lived experiences of some of the Black people in our industry, explaining what they feel is holding them back.

Justin Onuekwusi, Fund Manager

I've been running money since 2007 and am now relatively established as a fund manager, but this was not always the case. The first few years were really challenging. At my first big conference, which was full of financial advisors, there was a real buzz in the hall during the presentations: we had seen some great performance, had good momentum and decent asset growth over the years and received great feedback.

The good feeling soon ended though. In the evening there was the gala dinner, with fund managers sponsoring tables. I was a little bit late (which might not surprise some people!) and when I got to the table, some of the advisors were already sitting down. One of them looked up and said, 'Oh look, your twin is here.'

He pointed over to the other side of the room where there was another Black person. There were about 300 people...and he was pointing to the only other Black person in the room apart from me. The other guy was about fifty years old and, at the time, I was twenty-eight.

It's those kinds of things that reinforce the fact that you are an outsider. An imposter. There are lots of other stories like that which I could share, but that's the challenge that we know a lot of Black people face within the industry…just trying to feel like they belong.

Dawid Konotey-Ahulu, Business founder

When I went for my first job interview, they said: 'We really like you. We think you'd be a great fit here, and we'd love to offer you a job…but we can't.'

'Why not?' I asked.

'Well, we hired a Black guy last year and we can't just do it two years in a row. It's just something that we don't want to do.'

That's a kink in the hosepipe right there.

That was thirty years ago, but honestly, I'm not sure how much has changed. Earlier this year I was standing in the lobby in Angel Court in the City, where the firm that I co-founded is located on the sixth floor. I was talking to my chief financial officer right down on the ground floor by the escalators, and as we talked, almost everyone who walked into the building was showing me something.

It turned out that they were automatically showing me their passes. So we went and sat in Starbucks instead.

Last year, I was at a black-tie event where I was giving a speech. Just before dinner, a woman walks up to me and says: 'Do you think we could have another couple of bottles of white for the table?'

Speak to any of my Black friends; they will all, without exception, every one, tell you their story.

Gavin Lewis, Diversity Project Workstream Leader

The issues around race in this country are unique to the UK. The view is that we live in this post-racial society. You hear people saying, 'The UK doesn't have a problem with race.' Or, 'I haven't got a racist bone in my body.'

That's because the interpretation of racism is quite simplified. Cast your mind back to the murder of Stephen Lawrence in 1993. When that happened, Lawrence was eighteen – three years older than I was at the time. I was living in Tottenham and having to go to and from school in Enfield, which was then a National Front stronghold. So I was living the same nightmare. There were fights every day.

People think that the murder of Stephen Lawrence is what racism looks like – and yes, it can be violent and horrific. But that's not what we see so much of now. Racism has morphed.

When you go to organisations and talk about how you are going to increase ethnic-minority representation, as far as they're concerned the problem of racism (at least, what they think of as 'racism') doesn't exist. Ergo: the issue of race doesn't exist. The response is often to put out some well-meaning diversity and inclusion solutions – because they haven't unpacked what it is to be a Black person living in the UK.

So they do some good stuff. Recruit some Black people. Support #TalkAboutBlack. But until you really start to understand the lived experiences, you might get some diversity by having those people in your organisation...but the inclusion bit – where people really feel as if they belong – I think we're a step away from that.

There have been diversity and inclusion initiatives within the industry for over twenty years trying to address inequality, so why hasn't it worked for race? Part of it is very simple: the focus hasn't been on race. A lot of companies have taken the approach that they need to fix gender inequality first – and yes, women have had it much harder than men in the industry.

But another fact is this: men have women in their lives – mothers, sisters, partners, work colleagues. They know women. They are more comfortable with dealing with them. For many of the people I work with, I'm probably the only Black person that they know. If they are unfamiliar with Black people, how do you start unpacking issues that you don't even understand?

Dawid Konotey-Ahulu, Business founder

#TalkAboutBlack is not about Black vs privileged white per se. This is about asking for your help, everyone's help, to get rid of those kinks. Not because we're beggars or we're helpless. Not because we don't have our own ideas. Not that we don't have areas that we need to work on ourselves. But because it is impossible to change things by ourselves.

If everyone joins hands and comes alongside us, then we can change the system and we can improve ourselves. All of us. Every one of us. We're all part of the problem or part of the solution. There's no longer any safe middle ground. And when you do nothing, you're part of the problem.'

Inspired in part by the Diversity Project's panel discussions, my company ran a series of these towards the end of 2020. In the valuable discussion on ethnicity, some of our Black and Asian colleagues shared how their lives were affected by racism while they were growing up.

Pensions Administrator

As you get older, you begin to notice the little differences in how people will treat you. As a child you can't really figure out why these things happen... then it falls into place.

The first time I was really confronted with something like that was when I was with some friends as a teenager. We went into a shop and split up, as teenagers often do, and I noticed that – wherever I was walking – there was a security guard about five paces behind me. Not my friends. Just me. And I was the only Black person in that group.

I asked my mother why that had happened when I got home, and she said it was basically 'because you are Black'. It's the last thing that you want it to be, but when everything points to that answer, it's always at the back of your head. You just learn to live with it.

Sandra Hamberger, Personal Assistant

I had the usual name-calling as a child, but I let it go over my head. It was when my brother was attacked in the street by a group of five kids when he was seventeen and ended up in hospital for several days. It took four days for the police to come round and interview him. It was a very difficult time but, as a family, we pulled together.

The first time you become aware of it is in your formative years. So, it tends to be overt racism – being bullied and abused – rather than institutional racism. That tends to happen later.

When I was a student in France on my Erasmus year, whenever I went into the bank – a large international bank – I would have to show my ID, explain why I was there; all the while, local white French people were allowed to go on by me without being stopped. As you get older, you come to realise the institutionalised aspect of it.

Leading change to racial equality

The big message that comes through from these contributions is that most of us don't recognise what racism actually is or how it pervades our industry and society. Our perception of it, as Gavin Lewis points out, is based on a simplistic and outdated vision of open hostility towards Black people – not the less obvious, often 'unconscious' biases that shape our working practices.

Although getting involved in the Diversity Project can help to change some of the issues in the industry as a whole, our responsibility together is to make sure every company is open to anyone and that our culture is truly inclusive. In my company, we are making the following changes with this in mind:

- Facilitating discussion and guidance to staff on the different lived experience of minority groups to help a broader understanding of issues they may have faced

- Embedding the value of more cultural diversity, and driving better racial balance, in all areas of the business

- Developing a more ethnically diverse workforce through training and mentoring and encouraging more participation from ethnic minorities in our community

- Making inclusion a core priority for all employees, encouraging them to learn more about diversity and make inclusion a subconscious daily action

- Seeking new strong talent from a diverse range of racial and ethnic backgrounds

- Adding more content on diversity and inclusion to our induction training and the ongoing experience for employees during their time working for the business

- Being aware of unconscious bias and promoting inclusive leadership in development at all levels

- Building an understanding of ethnicity in the organisation and identifying areas for development

- Promoting an ethos where all are welcome

We have also signed up to the Business in the Community Race Charter,[38] which sets out five key areas of focus to ensure that ethnic-minority employees are represented at all levels in an organisation:

1. Appoint a specific person to lead on race in the company.

2. Track information on ethnicity and report publicly on progress.

3. Don't tolerate harassment or bullying, starting at the board level.

4. Make leaders and managers responsible for supporting equality.

5. Support employees in ethnic minorities to progress in their career.

Integrating these areas of focus into the culture of your business (not just paying lip service to them) is an imperative. It will force you to revaluate recruitment, retention, promotion, and learning and development processes to improve things for your existing employees and attract the people you want to work with in future.

Recruiting, nurturing and retaining Black talent

In his story, Gavin Lewis tellingly recounted just how difficult he found it to get past 'first base' in the investment and savings sector because, despite his qualities and qualifications, he didn't have the same advantages as his white peers. His degree wasn't from a Russell Group university. His student holidays were spent stacking shelves, not on an internship arranged by a family member or doing a Duke of Edinburgh award. He had to take a long, uncertain and circuitous route to get into an industry where he is now making a massive impact.

How many Gavin Lewises out there never get past the first obstacles, don't think that the industry would welcome them, or join and then become disillusioned about their career prospects because they come from backgrounds that are 'different' from those of the people around them?

Getting more Black people into the pipeline for our industry begins with taking positive action on the interns and graduates we bring in. Encourage internships from universities other than the usual suspects. Look beyond your usual 'tick boxes' at the interview stage. Just as establishing reverse mentoring between senior male and junior female employees builds bridges and encourages development, to retain Black talent you could set up mentoring that breaks down barriers that you might not recognise...because they aren't barriers you have faced.

Storytelling

Storytelling is a thread that runs through this book, because it's key to building bridges between people from different backgrounds in a business, breaking down barriers to inclusivity. Speaking from my experience, as well as that of other business managers I know, many people who are from a white background find it difficult to begin (let alone hold) a meaningful conversation with colleagues from an ethnic-minority background: they aren't sure what terms to use, or how to ask a question without sounding patronising, offensive or insensitive. Rather than risk offending a colleague, they never have that conversation.

Of course, not every Black person in your firm will want to talk about what being Black is like. Those who do, find themselves constantly having to rerun what might be a painful conversation. With that in mind, what's the best way to get your own #TalkAboutBlack conversation going? One way is to encourage people to talk about their lives, and let aspects such as their ethnicity come out as part of that if it is appropriate and comfortable. After all, we aren't defined by our ethnic background alone.

Several years ago, I introduced a short session at the beginning of each team meeting where everyone at the meeting could tell the others what was going on in their lives – professional and personal. People – junior and senior – began to talk about the challenges they were facing (childcare, looking after an elderly relative, struggling to work from home in a flat share, and so on). This has led to problems being shared, new (and sometimes seemingly unlikely) friendships being forged and a far more empathetic appreciation of the problems that can affect people's performance.

The benefits for team cohesion and collaborative working have been significant, and I've been able to address the challenges that employees faced before they felt the need to move job or leave the workplace. The extension of that, which has evolved as initial inhibitions have melted away, is that people are sharing more of their personal experiences in the form of extended stories, bringing specific issues to life by making it easier to relate to them.

I recommend that business managers encourage all staff members – including those from ethnic minorities – to share their stories, in whatever format works best for them and you.

The Diversity Project approach

The Diversity Project is working to 'unkink the hose' by inviting members to support or be involved in a four-stream action plan.

Pipeline

Challenge: UK Black-Caribbean and Black-African individuals experience higher rates of unemployment and are more likely to become victims of crime.

Solution: Creating an after-school programme to give secondary school children the knowledge, tools, connections and aspiration to enter the investments and savings industry.

Entry

Challenge: Even when Black individuals achieve a good education, they are less likely to be successful in securing their preferred roles; they are either not aware of asset management or not attracted to the industry because it seems to lack diversity.

Solution: Hosting an annual student event to identify and attract promising minority talent to the industry.

Progression

Challenge: When Black people do break into the industry, they typically end up in support roles, are more likely to leave and rarely progress to leadership or revenue-generating positions. At the time of writing, there are just thirteen Black portfolio managers, three Black heads of distribution and only two Black professionals in C-Suite positions.

Solution: Set up mentoring circles led by senior ethnic-minority professionals for those with up to ten years' experience; give business leaders a blueprint for increasing Black talent in their organisation.

Breaking the taboo

Challenge: People are generally comfortable with discussing issues relating to gender and sexual orientation, but race is still a taboo subject.

Solution: #TalkAboutBlack is breaking the taboo with thought leadership, roundtable debates, panel discussions, online videos, mainstream and trade media, and social media.

The CIPD perspective

The CIPD also has good advice on removing the barriers that stop Black and minority ethnic employees progressing to the top:

1. Understand what is happening in your organisation. Identify the structural and cultural barriers in your company that are maintaining inequalities.

2. Be aware of intersectionality and examine the barriers through multiple lenses. Many issues that affect the career progression of Black and minority ethnic employees are interconnected, so take account of this in your response.

3. Critically appraise your organisational culture. HR policies and processes that promote diversity and inclusion can set expectations, but they need to be regularly reviewed through a critical lens and underpinned by principles that actively celebrate and encourage differences.

4. Actively encourage 'employee voice' to inform change. Give employees ways to highlight issues

about inequality and express a view on matters affecting them at work.

5. Address unconscious bias. We all carry biases that we may not be aware of, but they affect our behaviour and decision-making.[39]

Gavin Lewis, Ethnicity Workstream Leader

I grew up on council estates in Tottenham with my mum and my sister; and, as a Black male growing up in Tottenham, the two main routes out were sport and music.

It was a very alpha male culture...a lot of violence and fighting...and until you come out of that and see the way other people live, you don't realise that this is not normal. Being so tall and gangly, I stood out like a sore thumb. I was always getting into fights.

I never really fitted in where I grew up, but I was good at two things. One was studying, the other was sports...and, luckily, sports let me hide the fact that I was a bit of a geek!

After experiencing some difficult situations, I decided quite early on that perhaps I could change my fortune and knuckled down to studying. I was fortunate to have a really strong mother who set an example. I saw her working late at night as a nurse, as well as studying to get into university, and that made a big impact on me.

So I studied. I got good grades at GCSE and A level and went to a good university, which took me out of my situation. But then I had no examples to follow in terms of the next stage. I thought that getting a good grade would be enough. I didn't realise that there was this whole other world of networking, sponsorship, work experience...and your face fitting.

There are many more Black graduates now who go to good universities and who are getting into the workplace: when I did that twenty years ago, I was a real anomaly. There was no guidance, no mentorship programme and no one like me who spoke out on this stuff. Just getting through the door was a problem. I had the grades, but I was told I wasn't 'rounded' like the other candidates. In their breaks from uni they'd been building wells in Africa or doing the Duke of Edinburgh. I'd been stacking shelves in Sainsbury's. But I did get told that I was 'really bright and articulate'. Why 'articulate' I've no idea...and I still hear that now.

How did you get where you are today?

After a few months, I decided to go into recruitment – not least because there appeared to be a lot of money to be made, and money was a big driver for me. I was working with asset managers and hedge-fund managers and thought, 'I could do that job'; so, I basically used my recruitment skills on myself for about six months, trying to get a break into the industry.

Eventually, a start-up firm took me on. Initially, it was a three-month contract – a way in that turned into a permanent role – but it was in 2007, and what we didn't foresee was the financial Armageddon in 2008, and there were times when I didn't even get paid. That was difficult, but I felt I had to stay to get a role with a bigger asset manager.

When I was working in recruitment one of my clients had been Russell Investments, and we'd kept in contact. I joined them for a few years as an institutional salesperson and then went to UBS, where I was promoted to executive director. Then I got approached by Vanguard, and on to BlackRock, where I've been since 2019.

I still often feel like a guest in the industry, and this has also been borne out by my peers…so I feel I have to watch what I say, how I say it, what I ask for, how I have discussions, my demeanour…Why? It's been a fight to get myself here, and there's almost a feeling that people are running a risk by taking me on; and that's left me – and others who've gone down the same road – somehow feeling we should be 'indebted' or 'grateful'.

Why did I get involved with the Diversity Project? Because I've always been a minority in the industry, breaking new ground – but never really belonging or fitting in…an 'outsider', seeing everything like an observer. I know it's not right, but you get used to it – and I felt like I could be a role model, setting an example just by being in the industry.

At first, I was a bit sceptical about the project: here's a bunch of middle-class white women...what do they know of my situation? Which shows you my own biases! But they've been the most supportive and inspirational group of people I've ever had the fortune to meet and work with, and the project has given us a real platform to voice our views on this issue.

Is the workstream making progress?

That depends on which day you catch me on! On days when I'm drained from trying to do all of this, I can say to my wife, 'I'm not sure that people really care about this,' and diversity becomes a tick box. But there are examples of where people have taken this personally and real change has happened. Some days I feel like diversity and inclusion doesn't work for minority groups – for ethnic minorities, in particular. Women still have a long way to go, but I think they can point to progress – although it's a very long time since the suffragettes first tied themselves to the railings! It works for women because the door wasn't flung open for them by men. They forced it open for themselves. There were enough of them to push against the door, and they also knew how the corporate world worked...they were familiar faces to the white male majority. And they had economic influence, the ability to set up pressure groups and get support.

If you look at where ethnic minorities are, we don't have any of that. There's just a handful of us. Very few of us went to a private school. And we're not familiar. I feel like I'm a guest at times, like I have to wear a mask.

On other days, I'm overwhelmed by how many people get in touch, inspired, saying, 'It's amazing what you've done – keep on.' So that's progress, and the fact that this book has been written shows it's on the agenda.

What are the benefits, and the challenges, of ethnic diversity?

I still think we have a long way to go in the industry, but for people like me it's a good time to be at the level I'm at. I've been saying this for years, but now I'm saying it with even more certainty: the world is changing, and what made something successful then won't make it successful in the future. You need people with different viewpoints, different perspectives, different life experiences. And ultimately, the world will hold us to account for society, our communities and the planet. The circumstances now [involvement in the Diversity Project] will mean that maybe people like me will be able to play a bigger role.

I'm not someone who's keen on the 'BAME' [Black and minority ethnic] tag, which groups everyone together. It's clearly an HR term to describe a group of people they don't know how to describe otherwise. For myself, I use the word 'Black'. I'm a Black person. And the diversity issue within the investment industry needs to be dissected, because some groups have done far better than others in gaining senior roles within the industry. Indians have done well, Bangladeshis and Pakistanis less so. Black Africans have done better than West Indians. There are a number of reasons for all of that, not least the aspirations that some communities have for their young people, and we are focusing on those groups that need the most help.

I think I've been fortunate in my career, because I've had sponsors who have really invested in me, but I also think that's because I'm a bit of an outlier. I've got to the position where I know what I'm doing in my job. I'm providing leadership. I look at these initiatives to improve gender and they are fantastic, because women need the investment. But I'm looking at them as a Black guy and thinking: 'Wouldn't it be great for us to have something like this?' Where it can become challenging is when diversity fatigue sets in and people start to think, 'OK, we've let the women in, now here come the gays. Now bringing up the rear, oh God, look there's some Black people. We're full!' That's my concern.

What needs to happen next?

Diversity solves one problem, because it's preparing the workplace to get the best out of people who maybe don't fit the mould. The problem is that when you think about ethnicity and socio-economic stats, you have all these structural barriers that have been built up over years and years.

So, diversity is just one leg of the stool. Access to education and social investment are the others, and all three legs of the stool need to be in place. You can go to a good school, but if when you get home in the evening you're looking after your brothers because your mum's working two shifts, you won't have time to do your homework.

We need to invest in those poorer areas and improve their economic fortunes. I've given a lot of thought to it, and I can't believe that the finance industry can't figure out ways to reduce inequality through what it invests in.

Five things to do

1. Actively pursue and recruit Black, Asian and ethnic minorities from universities you wouldn't normally consider.

2. Take an interest in the lives of the Black people in your organisation and invite them to share their stories with other employees and act as a 'champion'.

3. Establish a mentoring scheme in your business to help Black people progress – and to help white people understand their journeys.

4. Invite Black school children to visit your offices for a day (eg every quarter). Teach them essential

skills for a day. Ask your staff to sign up to the programme.

5. Tell your firm you care about this issue and why it matters. Put ethnicity on your board's agenda alongside other aspects of diversity, such as gender and sexuality.

THREE

Age

'There are different things that tend to happen to you at different stages of your life. In the early part of your career you may well be starting a family – and that can impact upon your work.'

   — Martin Hughes, Chief Technology Officer[40]

Challenges and issues

If you want a workforce that truly represents a wide spectrum of cognitive diversity, you have to employ people of all ages.

'No problem,' I hear many people say. 'We've got people working from us aged from eighteen to sixty-eight. That's a fifty-year spread of diverse thinking and lived experiences.' That may well be true, but where do those people sit in your organisation? Inevitably, older age will reflect seniority – and unless certain mechanisms are in place, the old hierarchical model can make it hard (or even impossible) to build the sort of diverse teams that now drive our businesses.

Management structures today need to be far more flexible to allow different (younger) ways of thinking to penetrate the senior management echelons. They need to encourage a good flow of young people to join the business – and to stay – in an era when most younger people look to change jobs every year or two. Employers need to have working practices that make it possible for people to stay in their job while they're raising a family; those people need to feel they can still forge a career, not just tread water. Managers need to recognise that, to retain the talents and experience of many older people, they will need to make some compromises about the work/life balance on offer. Above all, to build teams that include people from all age groups requires a management approach that lets these groups blend seamlessly, work cohesively and give their best.

Writing from experience, some fairly nifty footwork is needed to keep everyone on board and motivated, as well as functioning to the best of their ability. In *Manage The Gap*, you can find much more detail about how to recruit, retain and manage intergenerational teams. In this book, the focus is on specific groups: young talent, women returning to the workforce, and 'working families'.

To encourage age-related diversity in your company, it's important to be aware of the challenges that employees may face at different stages of life:

- Older employees may want to scale down their role or their hours for health reasons or to achieve a better work/life balance. They may also have caring responsibilities to juggle.

- Those in mid-career may need guidance and support to determine how best to spend their remaining years with the business, including by retraining or changing roles.

- Women returning to the workforce may need to go part time or stagger their return so they can continue providing childcare.

- Many fathers now want to play a major part in their children's early years, so they may need more flexibility too.

- Women going through the menopause may need support or flexible working.

There is one overarching message: employers need to recognise that (increasingly) people expect to have a life outside work, and to attract certain groups, flexibility and 'smart working' (more on this in Chapter Six) will need to be priorities, not perks.

Lived experiences

As part of a panel discussion on age diversity, a member of our technology team told the following story about the challenges he faced when he was trying to juggle a demanding role with caring for an elderly relative. This experience will resonate with many employees in middle age.

Martin Hughes, Chief Technology Officer

There are different things that tend to happen to you at different stages of your life. In the early part of your career you may well be starting a family – and that can impact upon your work. Round about when I was turning fifty, my mum (who was in her early nineties), living alone, 200 miles away, was not in very good shape at all. She really should have been having daily care, but she was refusing it and trying to muddle through and make do. Things got progressively worse, and I'm 200 miles away trying to manage that. That can take away your attention from work.

Things progressed, she had a fall, broke her leg and ended up in hospital. She had various other health conditions – cancer, Alzheimer's and other difficult challenges that she was facing. I had to get involved more and more, arranging hospital visits, sorting out a care home. Often, on a Friday afternoon I would find myself on a train up to the north-west for a meeting with doctors or carers to solve the next problem for Mum.

Luckily, I had colleagues and a boss who were very understanding and accommodated my occasional absences and lapses of focus. In the end, she went into a care home which was really nice and suited her until the end of her life. But how much harder that would all have been if that support network had not been in place.

There are some subtle differences in what the different generations look for from their managers. The younger cohorts, for example, expect a lot more reassurance and 'hand holding' – which was rarely forthcoming in my early years in the industry. In our panel discussion around age, our graduate trainee Beth Pugh made the following point:

'If I don't get feedback, I start to panic: "Oh my God, am I doing it wrong? Is that why they haven't said anything?"

'Even if you're not doing something right, or you could do something better, if you're not hearing back on that... you can't improve. Just having feedback opens up the conversation with a manager, so you're more willing to say what's on your mind. Regular conversations are definitely important to me.'

I would go further and argue that regular conversations are important for *every* member of your team. Never assume that the way you were managed twenty or thirty years ago will work today.

Leading change to age equality

The population is ageing, with life expectancy rising and fewer younger people entering work. Traditionally, the investment and savings sector has 'cut loose' many older employees well before state pension age to accommodate younger people in the senior ranks and reduce longer-term defined benefits pension commitments. This practice has not served the sector well, with firms often jettisoning the wholesale experience, soft skills and contacts of older workers.

Demographic changes are putting pressure on future talent pools. In their 2017 report, the Local Government Association estimated that by 2024 there will be a shortage of over four million people to meet the demand for high-skilled jobs.[41] To fill that gap, look no further than the increasing availability of older people in the general population thanks to the 'Boomer birth bulge' during the 1950s and 1960s. Many people in this generation are not only able to carry on working into their sixties, seventies or beyond but also want (or need) to carry on being economically active. Their skills, experience and knowledge can complement the talents of younger employees.

In spite of this, many employers are still giving experienced employees incentives to retire early or letting them leave without finding ways to retain them, even part time or as consultants. This can cost the business a vast amount of expertise and knowledge, while casting aside people with thirty or even forty years of life ahead who aren't prepared, psychologically and often financially, for their new situation.

It is possible to retain (and retrain, if needed) these older employees while still promoting younger talent and containing costs. The rest of this chapter explains how.

Why an intergenerational workforce works best

The biggest reason to retain older people in your workforce is the cognitive diversity they can bring to your team. How, though, might this look in practice? And how do you overcome the often-marked variations in approach that different generations have towards work?

Few of us fit precisely into a mould defined by our date of birth, but every generation has broad characteristics, shaped by the cultural influences and social-economic pressures that prevailed in our formative years. Blending these characteristics in a team can provide the talent, knowledge and range of perspectives needed for a company to manage change, seize new opportunities and rise to challenges.

As with any team, the 'players' in different generations should be encouraged to work to their strengths. Younger members may appear to be more comfortable with the latest technology; they may be keen to try out new ways of doing things. Older members may have the soft skills of dealing with people, years of knowing what does (and doesn't) work, strategic thinking, a deep knowledge of the industry, and contacts. Put all of these characteristics into a diverse team and you have the potential for the perfect fusion. Remember that, as your client base ages with the rest of the population, having an age-diverse team is a good way to match the profile of your customers and deliver products and services that will resonate with them.

Plenty of research backs up this positive picture. In 2014, The CIPD published *Managing an Age-diverse Workforce: Employer and employee views.*[42] It showed that employees valued the benefits of working with colleagues of different ages in the following order of importance: knowledge sharing (55%), customer service (14%), improved problem-solving (9%) and greater innovation (7%). One in five (20%) pointed to the benefits of greater innovation and enhanced customer service delivery.

Retaining older employees in a way that works for everyone

One of the challenges for older employees is that work may not be the only call on their time and energy. Large numbers have caring responsibilities for partners, older relatives or grandchildren. Many want to start reducing their working week to enjoy a better work/life balance or accommodate health conditions that make it problematic to work at the level they are used to.

Traditional career structures are changing, and at some point in life – for example, when reaching a significant age – people will want to stop, re-evaluate, and think about taking time out to pursue other interests or explore other avenues. 'Cliff-edge' retirement will be a thing of the past. Expect less of a canalised waterway (study, first job, series of promotions, retirement) and more of a meandering river, complete with the odd oxbow lake (eg study, first job, promotions, return to study, second career, wind down, become self-employed, semi-retire). This opens up the opportunity for us all to enjoy fuller, richer lives, but it also throws up challenges. How will people negotiate changes with their employer or go about job hunting or retraining? How will they finance the years ahead if they are going to work less or in less-well-paid roles?

Enter the 'midlife review', sometimes referred to as a 'midlife MOT', which is the subject of my second book, *The Midlife Review: A guide to work, wealth and wellbeing.*[43]

The concept has gained significant traction in recent years – not least because the government is keen on the benefits that longer working lives bring to the national economy: reduced dependency on state benefits and increased tax revenues and gross domestic product.

Not to be confused with the regular career reviews that many employers provide, the midlife review focuses on the medium to long term and looks at a person's situation holistically. It's the starting point for deeper reflection on finances, work aspirations and overall wellbeing. In short, everything that can impact upon a person's work is (ideally) examined, with a view to developing a clear perspective on what will enable them to be their best at work, for themselves and their employer – even if that means going part time, changing role, winding down to retirement or leaving entirely. Rather than being a way of trying to gently edge someone out, the overriding objective is to retain the talents and experience of older people in the workforce by identifying the right course to meet their needs and aspirations.

How a midlife review can work

A midlife review should drill right down to an individual's personal and professional drivers: their ambitions, health and finances. The three key questions to ask are:

1. What do *you* want to achieve in the coming phases of your life – and if you could choose,

what would be the role and working patterns you'd prefer, and the life you would like to lead outside work?

2. Do you – or when will you – have the funds in place to live that life? Having looked at the figures, do you need to adjust your plans or how much you are saving?

3. Will your health support your future aspirations, or might you need to adjust your wellbeing and fitness regime to ensure it doesn't start to cause problems?

Work, wealth and wellbeing are the three legs that support a midlife review, and exploring them in more depth gives a person the opportunity to look ahead and take control of their future. An open conversation with an employer or consultant can help answer the first question. A financial consultant will have the planning tools to produce a range of scenarios to show when (or if) they can afford to drop back on their hours, take on a different role or even retire. Many employers encourage their staff or even fund them to have a thorough health check to answer the third question.

Making the midlife review work for employers and employees

The biggest message from all the research and pilot schemes to date is that there is no 'one size fits all'. Companies should look at the elements that have worked well elsewhere, create a template that would work best for them, and test that template with a small group before rolling it out across the business.

It might also be useful to bring in consultants or advisors for some elements or make use of the specialists you already have to hand.

Age equality at other stages of life

To promote age equality in your company, it's important to meet the work-related needs of groups of people who are experiencing challenges associated with particular stages of life. Two of these are women going through the menopause and working families.

Menopause

The average age of menopause is fifty-one,[44] but it can happen any time from the thirties to the mid-fifties – or sometimes even later. Every woman will experience symptoms differently; some will have fewer or less severe symptoms, while others will have more regular and significant symptoms. In our panel discussions, one of our administrators described the challenges she faced at work while going through the menopause:

'I started experiencing menopausal symptoms just after my fortieth birthday, which, to start with, I would not believe was the menopause

because I was so young. None of my friends
were experiencing this and my mother had
died a few years earlier, so I had no one close
to discuss it with. At work, my manager was
a woman younger than me and I did not feel
comfortable discussing it with her. The reality
was that I really struggled at work because
my mind was often foggy and hot flushes
came from nowhere, which made me feel
very self-conscious and uncomfortable. In
hindsight, it would have been so much easier
if I could have had a conversation and some
understanding from my manager.'

Here are the most common symptoms of the menopause:

- Psychological issues, such as mood disturbances,
  anxiety, depression, memory loss, panic attacks,
  loss of confidence and reduced concentration

- Hot flushes (brief and sudden surges of heat,
  usually in the face, neck and chest)

- Night sweats (hot flushes during the night)

- Sleep disturbance, which may make people feel
  tired and irritable

- Irregular periods, or periods that are lighter or
  heavier than usual

- Muscle and joint stiffness, aches and pains

- Urinary tract infections, including cystitis

- Headaches

- Weight gain

- Palpitations (heartbeats that become more noticeable)

- Skin changes (dryness, acne, general itchiness)

- Reduced sex drive[45]

The CIPD recommends that employers can do the following things to help someone with menopause symptoms to carry on doing their job:[46]

1. Keep an open mind and avoid making assumptions about someone's condition or how it may be affecting their ability to do their job.

2. Treat every employee as an individual, because menopause symptoms can vary hugely from person to person.

3. Adjustments can be physical, such as providing a fan, but they can also involve changes such as offering a more flexible working arrangement.

4. Menopause symptoms can fluctuate, so take a flexible approach and check in regularly with the person.

Working families

There are various ways to define a 'working family'; for the purposes of this book, it's any single person or couple trying their best to combine work with caring responsibilities. That definition overlaps with many other 'groups', but there are some specific challenges for achieving a work/life balance when you have the pressure of holding down (let alone advancing) a career while a family member is relying on you or you're providing parental care.

Many of us will find ourselves grappling with this situation at some stage in our working life, and not just if we have children: the challenge that many carers of elderly relatives face is set to become more significant in the years ahead as the population ages and formal support networks come under more pressure. How employers help people deal with these situations can prove critical. It was certainly a challenge that has special relevance to my own career. Indeed, I might not have progressed as far as I have without my employer's support.

In 2002, the UK company I had been working for had recently been acquired by a US business, and this posed a problem. I had young children and wanted to play as full a part as I could in their early years. I had previously negotiated that I would work from home but come in once or twice a week at times that suited me. However, the US business wanted me in the office every day – because that was how they worked.

As a compromise, we agreed that I could come into the office each day at 7.30am and leave at 4pm. That would, at least, allow me to get home in time to bath the children and put them to bed. I had gone from what was (at the time) a flexible UK employer to a rigid US one; but I had been given some sort of compromise, even if it meant a daily two-hour commute.

Each day when I left at four, all I got from my colleagues was abuse about 'working half days', despite the fact that I'd put in an hour and a half ahead of them. It was that experience that led me, at the age of thirty-two, to give up my London salary and set up as a self-employed individual working from home. It meant a big drop in income, but I could walk my children to pre-school, pick them up and be with them for a few hours each evening...working furiously in between. I managed to maintain that regime for five years before the business started to grow – and I got sucked back into working in an office again.

Because I wanted to be part of my children's lives at a time that was hugely important for bonding, my only option was to leave the company. Would that still be the case? You would think that in the twenty years since, the industry would have moved on to accommodate male and female employees who are balancing a career with raising a young family.

When I faced that challenge, much of the pressure came from my peers; but that was because it was the prevailing culture, and a company's culture stems from the top. They were still going out for beers after work and couldn't understand why I didn't want to join them on a Thursday, effectively choosing the family over them. If the employer cared, they'd stamp on that sort of thing. I certainly would if I saw it going on today.

The Diversity Project approach

Although the issue of retaining older employees is not yet a separate workstream for the Diversity Project, the other workstreams are contributing to ensuring that our industry has an age-diverse workforce in the future.

Early careers

Each year, thousands of young people enter the investment and savings industry from university – but the majority of them have graduated from just a handful of institutions. Most are from families who have either contacts or a background in the sector; or who, because they are relatively well off, are well versed in how the sector works.

What happens to the tens of thousands of talented young people who don't have this background or 'leg up'? Many are being lost to the sector at the first hurdle: they either never apply or get knocked back at the CV stage. Trying to open up the pool of potential talent is the focus of the Early Careers workstream, led by Shruti Khandekar and Emma Douglas. As they make clear here, they have decided that a narrow focus can achieve the best results in the short term.

Shruti Khandekar (former) and Emma Douglas, Early Careers Workstream Leaders

Our workstream has been going for four years now, and rather than try and cover all of the factors that can hinder young people from different backgrounds coming into the sector in one go – such as gender, ethnicity or neurodivergence – we're focusing on just one big cross-cutting issue in the first instance: social mobility. Critically, we felt this was a hidden problem, one which companies probably aren't even aware of because the data to demonstrate that young people from disadvantaged backgrounds aren't making it through – especially to revenue-generating functions – isn't always captured.

Neither of us come from a 'disadvantaged' background in the classic sense of the word, but we did go to state schools and didn't have any family background in the sector. Unaware of all the different opportunities in the industry, we both had to work that much harder to find out about it and be successful 'fitting in' when we did so. It must be even tougher for students who don't have the emotional support and push towards education that both our families could offer us.

The demographic we are targeting is first- and second-year university students from state schools rather than private schools – in particular, those from lower socio-economic demographic backgrounds who wouldn't have been exposed to the investment and savings industry growing up because of their family backgrounds and education, and so probably would never even consider it as a career.

Our aim is to identify them early on in their university careers – ideally their first year – gain their interest and broaden their knowledge of the sector, provide mentoring and support with getting internships and interviews, and give them the tools they will need to be taken on by companies on graduating. Most importantly, we want to support them in building the confidence to apply for roles and do as well in interviews as their more resourced peers.

As with all the workstreams, we have to recognise what we can do on our own…and when we should be reaching out for specialist help. We could see early on that we didn't have the contacts or the resources to identify suitable young people, so over 2019 we developed a programme in partnership with a social mobility charity called upReach,[47] whose mission is 'to help disadvantaged students from across the UK to realise their potential'. They already know the relevant societies on campus and careers officers, and how to access the relevant young people by asking the right questions. They can bring students from across the country into a common pool, filtered by socio-economic status. They also provide the crucial pastoral support for the students, in addition to the support the students will receive from their mentor.

There are successful programmes – like Investment 20/20, run by the Investment Association – which are already working well across schools and in supporting the non-university routes into the investment sector. The same breadth of diversity in young hires has not yet found its way into the 'traditional' internship and graduate roles, which require undergraduate degrees. Furthermore, for the latter roles, when companies do move away from the usual universities to attract a wider range of students, the tendency is to go to the other end of the spectrum and try to find students from disadvantaged backgrounds, or provide support at an earlier stage in the education process (to sixth-formers) in the most disadvantaged areas. That's not wrong for a moment, but the cultural challenge of bringing in somebody from an environment where they may even struggle to finish school is quite difficult. I think we can be more successful if we go to the 'missed middle' group of universities – which are good ones, but maybe with students from a slightly different background and who bring a perspective not reflected in the industry today.

Is progress being made?

The programme is going well. Students take part in a series of events across the first year, designed to give them a better understanding of the industry and the different roles available. Alongside that, each student gets a mentor from a firm who helps them with mock interviews and CVs, and provides any general support required – whether with applications or even understanding workplace etiquette.

We also hold an 'Academy' – two days of events, exercises and speakers to build students' technical investment knowledge and soft skills. The programme then concludes with an awards ceremony to celebrate the students' success over the year.

For the first year, we had over twenty-five firms involved in some way or another, supporting around a hundred students from thirty-six different UK universities, who have been filtered by upReach. Some have completed successful virtual internships; the rest are still in mentoring or early stages.

Unfortunately, Covid-19 hampered an in-person work-experience week for the students. However, several firms were able to provide successful virtual work-experience weeks in the summer of 2020. It is likely the work-experience week in 2021 will also be virtual for the new cohort of students. Although it was a shame that the students weren't able to get a flavour of what it's like to work in an office, something that many will never have experienced before, it was great to see how quickly the firms were able to make the work experience virtual so the cohort did not miss out on this really important opportunity.

From the initial pilot scheme with 100 students, we have now increased this to 170 students in total across our first and second year of the programme. We are continuing to support the first cohort of students – they maintain a mentoring relationship and attend virtual sessions to keep up to date on key developments in the industry. We're also rerunning the first year of the programme with new students, albeit all virtually. It's fantastic to have yet more firms (over 30), mentors (from 100 to 170) and volunteers involved in the programme, with enthusiasm and support for it growing as well.

We can't guarantee that these students will get jobs, but we're giving them work experience to put on their CVs and so at least they'll get through the door. You can't tell firms to take these students, but they do have a better chance of their potential being seen. Over time, that provides an opportunity to address the disproportionate situation we now see. We're confident that by equalising the opportunities on offer to all undergraduates in the UK (rather than targeting an equalised outcome), we will find no shortage of talented, capable students whose perspectives and drive bring in the diversity that this industry needs if it is to continue to be successful.

What can firms do to tap into this talent pool?

1. Be open-minded at the CV and interview stages. Look beyond the usual colleges and the practised polish, and recognise that someone from a

red-brick university may have all the talent and energy – and has had to work harder to get there.

2. Try to think how you can get the best group of people, not just the 'best people'. You don't need to hire twenty graduates who all want to be the next CEO. You only need one or two of them. If you had to recruit a cohort of graduates or interns, what different skill sets do they need? Taking that approach would build in the diversity that would make your organisation better.

3. Try to break the (natural) inclination to appoint someone like you. Look at someone with a different experience of life: that's what you need to avoid groupthink in your business.

4. Consider the benefits to clients. We all have different clients now – they aren't just white, middle-aged men. We need people who can get the best outputs tailored to their needs, and who can better reflect the person opposite them.

5. Look at your job specs. Many companies make a maths or economics degree a default, but in lots of roles you don't need beyond A-level maths. Rethink what the actual skill requirements are before you set the bar.

6. Look at the transferable skills that the candidate has, such as those acquired from part-time jobs and voluntary work, and consider which might be useful to your business.

Working families

I also spoke to Claire Black and Sascha Calisan, who lead the Diversity Project's Working Families workstream, about their challenges of being a parent while pursuing a career which is very different from my own and what employers could do to change organisational culture and remove barriers to working parents.

Claire Black and Sascha Calisan, Working Families Workstream Leaders

What are the challenges that you've faced as working parents?

Sascha: I was in a similar situation to Claire, in having multiple miscarriages over the course of seven years, and became physically ill as a result of trying to work my way through it. There were times when I'd be in hospital, having had a miscarriage, on a work call making a presentation. It was bonkers, but I didn't want them to know that I was pregnant, or thinking about becoming pregnant.

I got myself really ill with chronic fatigue. After a while, my GP signed me off. After two months I went back to her, she asked me how I was, and I said: 'A bit better, but now I'm pregnant...' 'Right,' she said. 'You're absolutely going to have this one,' and signed me off for another three months. I did have the baby, but the little monkey came out eight weeks early, so I had problems at the other end as well!

Because of the way women have been perceived in the workplace, you don't want to acknowledge that you're trying to have a family. And a lot of the reason why women are having fertility issues is because of the additional stresses involved. What's the advice here? One is always anxious about mentioning pregnancy for the first three months to anyone, let alone your employer, because of the elevated risk of miscarriage.

Sascha: There are a lot of conflicting issues here, but I think there just has to be more openness, that 'this is us'. Everybody's affected by it. The majority of people at some time in their lives are going to be building a family, and it's just got to become part of the supported norm in the workplace.

Claire: And, obviously if you are having fertility treatment, you need to let your employer know, as you will need time out of work. However, another difficulty is because you're making yourself vulnerable, suddenly you can find yourself not being given the opportunities.

How easy was it for you to get your careers back on track?

Sascha: My experience at this point was different from Claire's. Our children are the same age, but I wasn't a single parent when I returned. I went back in a flexible way – one day working from home at first, then building up to two days at home, and I did 8am until 4pm so I could fit in childcare.

I work at a US Bank and they have one of the best family-friendly policies and are always trying to improve them. There was a lot of support for the practicalities.

When you are constrained in time, you are very focused on getting your head down and doing the job in hand: you won't find many people coming back from maternity leave and not delivering. In fact, they become a very efficient and actually more effective member of the workforce in many ways. They can't do the list of twenty things they'd normally do, so they focus on the really important things.

But one thing that women often don't do as well as men in normal times is the networking. Men will naturally find ways to network, while women are more reticent. And when you're time-constrained, that doesn't happen at all. I'm trying to mentor women to take out at least half an hour a week and reach out to somebody they're not working with…whether that's having a coffee, or whatever. You owe it yourself to do that.

You forget about yourself because suddenly you are all about your child, and getting home and doing that family time. Your career is almost bottom of the list. You do your job because you need the income, and you do it well. Then, when you have more time because they are in school, and you're ready for your next step up, no one thinks about you because you're not on their radar. You've just been a 'steady performer'.

The importance of taking that time, having that coffee, thinking strategically, making sure people know what you're working on…all that goes to the bottom of women's lists. It's not just about the tools that employers give you to come back to work – flexible working, emergency childcare – but also what you need to keep your career path going.

One of the things my employer did well was a maternity leave returner course, and it included creating your own brand. We're now talking about having a mentor even before you go off on maternity leave, to keep the lights on. All that said, even now I'm back and doing well, I feel as though I lost five years.

Should companies be doing more to facilitate networking – inside and outside the company?

Claire: It's a combination of encouraging networking to keep you current and connected, and mentoring to make sure you are doing all the right things. It doesn't have to be a huge investment in time, just making sure people are doing it.

What is the root of the problem?

Sascha: You might have the best HR policies on flexible working, but it does come down to the individual managers. And I know female managers who work flexibly themselves but won't let their teams work flexibly. It's not just men; it's females doing it to other females. It can be a lack of perspective, and some of it must be around trust. Covid-19 has now made people realise just how many jobs can be done flexibly. If it's a problem with your manager then they too need some form of support, as they have not always had the experience of people returning from maternity leave.

Coming back after a year can almost be like starting a new job again; it's just that you happen to know the people! It's a lot of information to take in, and when your brain capacity is not firing on all cylinders it's really exhausting. Your manager needs to know what you're going through if they are to give you the support you need and to help you work in a way that would be most effective for you and for them. And they need to listen when you have that conversation.

Is 'working families' a male challenge as well as a female one?

Sascha: When we set the scope for this workstream, we felt it was really important to bring in the working dads, as dads taking paternity leave bring a whole load of different issues...not least, the whole debate around whether or not it's the 'done thing'. Maybe Covid-19 has pushed that forward, but there aren't enough men doing it, and often the dad is the higher income earner.

We have split the workstreams: one looking at the challenges that women face; the other at paternity leave and, specifically, shared parental leave. Where it can be made to work, it's fantastic in terms of shared careers, the dad being involved from the outset.

Will the lessons learned during Covid-19 help you get to where you want quicker?

Sascha: It has accelerated flexible working, and positive management attitudes towards that are a big part of what working families need to combine both roles. To have men put on their out-of-office email that they are not available 'as they are providing childcare' is just so fantastic. Execs now realise that you *are* productive working from home, not skiving or doing the laundry. It's done wonders on that side.

Claire: All the pressures that working families come under were really highlighted during lockdown. We didn't have to get into the office, but we still had to juggle work and looking after our children throughout the day, and keeping their education going too. It really showed just how dependent we are upon having structures in place to make achieving the balance possible.

Looking forward, what needs to happen for employers to support working families?

Sascha: We've demonstrated that things can be done differently – now it's important that conversations are held, that mentoring is made available, and ways are found to make it work for them as well as the employee.

Claire: It's important to remember that it's not a 'one size fits all'. Line managers need to be in touch with each of their staff's personal situations, because

INCLUSIVE CULTURE

otherwise they can't begin to understand. The other side of it is that employees have to come forward too – like Sascha, I'm not always very good at saying what my situation is. If your line manager isn't in tune with the fact that there's something going on for you, or doesn't ask you the question, they'll assume that you're fine.

Sascha: Part of it is down to trust, as well as understanding. When I went back to work eight years ago, the manager assumed that I would be having a fairly easy time, as I was working flexibly. Part of it is organisation. Part of it is peer support, and mentoring groups can be especially helpful for getting people through issues such as menopause…which is another thing people don't want to talk about! And, really, it's about all areas of life. We need people to come together and openly talk about these things as challenges that most of us will face at some point, and to help each other.

It's about treating each person as an individual with a life outside work. It's about employers looking after that whole circle of life.

The CIPD perspective

The CIPD offers the following advice to employers who want to lead change to age equality:

1. Offer a midlife review for people aged fifty or over.

2. Promote flexible working for all age groups.

3. Take a strategic approach to workforce planning to understand the future skills requirement for the business so that employees of all ages can be trained appropriately.

4. Review recruitment processes and policies to avoid bias which may be preventing people from applying for roles.

5. Develop a culture of lifelong learning across the business to ensure everyone regardless of ages continues to develop.

6. Promote employee wellbeing.

7. Discuss various retirement options with older workers so that all alternatives can be considered by the individual and the business.[48]

Five things to do

1. Look at the older members of your company and ask yourself: who is likely to still be here in five years' time, how easy will it be to replace them and what gaps will that leave?

2. Set up midlife reviews for all staff aged fifty and over – and make them regular events, because people's situations change.

3. Put flexible working at the heart of everything you do, and engage all your staff in the process – especially senior team members, who might find the concept alien.

4. Broaden your intern and graduate recruitment processes to encourage students and graduates from a wider range of demographic backgrounds and universities.

5. Set up a 'working family' networking group in your company. This will allow employees (male and female) to share experiences and knowledge, and provide them with a united platform to discuss how they can establish working practices that work for you and them.

FOUR

Ability

'People with disabilities have found themselves, for a long time, almost second-class citizens right across the world.'

— Katy Halliday, Disability Workstream Leader[49]

Challenges and issues

The definition of disability is somewhat wide and may not always be obvious. Government guidance about the Equality Act 2010 states you are disabled if:

- You have a physical or mental impairment

- That impairment has a substantial and long-term adverse effect on your ability to carry out normal day-to-day activities[50]

The critical word is 'impairment', which does not necessarily mean a medical condition and the emphasis is very much on the impairment of a person's ability to do day-to-day activities.

Some impairments are automatically treated as a disability:

- Cancer
- Visual impairment (certified as blind, severely sight-impaired, sight-impaired or partially sighted)
- Multiple sclerosis
- HIV infection
- Severe, long-term disfigurement

And some impairments are explicitly excluded:

- Seasonal allergic rhinitis (hay fever)
- Tattoos and ornamental body piercings
- Various antisocial personality disorders
- Addictions to alcohol, nicotine or other substances (which are not covered unless the addiction was originally the result of medical treatment or medically prescribed drugs)

However, impairments such as a learning difficulty, dyslexia or autism could be considered a disability under the Equality Act depending on how it affects a person's day-to-day life.

Considering all these factors, some 8.4 million (20%) of working age adults in the UK live with a limiting long-term illness, impairment or disability.[51] Significantly, 3.6 million disabled people of working age are economically inactive. The unemployment rate is 8.4% compared to 4.6% for people who are not disabled. The government has been working to promote the employment prospects of people with disabilities and health conditions through its Disability Confident campaign which highlights the employer benefits:

- Draw from the widest possible pool of talent increasing the number of high-quality applicants.

- Secure high-quality staff who are skilled, loyal and hard working.

- Improve employee morale and commitment by demonstrating that you treat all employees fairly.

- Create a diverse workforce that reflects the customers it serves and communities that it is based around.[52]

Cognitive diversity

If 'cognitive diversity' is a management aim, neurodiversity has to play a role. Neurodiversity is the infinite variation in how our brains are 'wired'.[53] From an organisational point of view, these variations in cognitive functioning can increase diversity of thought and reduce groupthink. It also provides ready access to sought-after skills: the more neurodiversity we have in our business, the more able we are to look at things in a different way and question established ways of thinking and working.

The neurological set-up of people with (for example) autism, attention deficit hyperactivity disorder (ADHD) or dyslexia results in many distinct qualities – ranging from creative thinking to process structuring. When we understand and value this potential, we can access a world of opportunities.

The word 'neurodiversity' was first used in the late 1990s by journalist Harvey Blume and autism advocate Judy Singer. In 1998, Blume wrote in *The Atlantic*:

> 'Neurodiversity may be every bit as crucial for the human race as biodiversity is for life in general. Who can say what form of wiring will prove best at any given moment?'[54]

In his book *The Power of Neurodiversity: Unleashing the advantages of your differently wired brain*, Dr Thomas Armstrong writes:

> 'Dyslexics, for example, can be seen in terms of their visual thinking ability and entrepreneurial strengths. People with ADHD can be regarded as possessing a penchant for novel learning situations. Individuals along

the autistic spectrum can be looked at in terms of their facility with systems such as computer programming or mathematical computation.'[55]

At the moment, most work environments and practices are distinctly geared against someone with a neurodivergent brain: our hiring processes, management techniques and workplace procedures have been created by and for neurotypical brains. Even if the person gets past the interview process, they are likely to find the 'traditional' way of working antipathetic to the way they can best function.

Neither has it been a helpful assumption in society as a whole to equate neurodiversity with impaired mental health: they are not the same. That said, neurodivergent individuals may be more prone to certain disorders than the general population. For example, anxiety disorders have a high prevalence among individuals on the autism spectrum.[56] In part, this can be attributed to the challenges and frustrations experienced when trying to navigate a neurotypical world.

To retain the talents of neurodivergent people, employers need to understand and recognise potential barriers and, where necessary, design them out of the person's work environment. The good news is that more firms are now recognising the importance of neurodiversity in the workplace by bringing a different way of thinking to teams.

Lived experiences

Richard Hawkins, Employee Benefit Consultant

I am registered disabled by virtue of being sight-impaired, so what that means for me is that I have a degenerative eye defect where I am aggressively losing my peripheral vision and in later years will lose a lot of my central vision. It started in my early teens as night blindness and in my thirties, it has developed into tunnel vision, so the rule of thumb is if I am looking directly at something I can see it but otherwise I cannot see it, which can create problems.

I particularly struggle in low light conditions which means in dusk and pre dusk I struggle to see things, which as a Scot that means six months of the year. I have needed to make some adjustments at work. Thankfully I work with a great bunch of people who understand that I cannot see very well and acknowledge that I am likely to walk into them at any given moment. Most of my clients are aware and have made adjustments for me. I do undertake a mini risk assessment myself when I visit clients to ensure I keep safe – I have learned from painful experience that I need to ensure cables and chairs are tucked away because if I can, I will fall over them.

My main worry is my later life, as I don't want to be a burden on my family. I also have just had a little girl and I don't want Katharine to go through some of the stuff I have been through if she develops the same sight issues. I need to be a good role model for her so she understands that this does not have to be a big deal and as a disabled person she should not be treated any differently.

Subira Jones, Burnout Prevention Consultant and Lifestyle Coach, draws on her own and other people's experience to explain why it's so important to make flexible working options available to employees with disabilities.

Subira Jones, Burnout Prevention Consultant and Lifestyle Coach

Being a woman of Jamaican descent with a degree in economics, I appreciate the great strides taken to expand diversity in the investment and savings industry, allowing me to pursue the career of my choice – irrespective of race and gender. However, my medical condition has meant that I have met other barriers and led directly to me leaving my role as a client reporting analyst and pursuing a career as a burnout prevention consultant and lifestyle coach, with the vision of helping other talented professionals avoid burnout and debilitating work stress illnesses.

My experiences demonstrate just how difficult it is for anyone with a disability or chronic health condition to fulfil their potential within the sector without one critical factor being available to them: flexibility. And, with some 20% of the population having some form of disability, 96% of which are 'invisible', just how many talented people are currently not coming into the sector simply because of employers' inflexibility (real or perceived) around part-time and home working? How many are not moving on to more challenging roles because they can't negotiate the same flexible terms they have negotiated in their current job?

That's why I was delighted to become a Diversity Project ambassador. I call myself The Corporate Hippie™ because that's the juxtaposition between my analytical side (I enjoy working in the investment world) and being people-centred in how I do things. I've always felt I was a round peg in a square hole...but on the right board.

I took my degree at Swansea, but in my final year my mother suffered a heart attack and went into a coma. I finished my degree, then came back to London to spend some critical time with her. I wasn't in a position to take on a full-time, demanding job so I opted to waitress, which allowed me to earn a living and have the flexibility to visit my mum in hospital.

My mother remained severely neurologically disabled, so in 2017, two years later, I decided it was time to get a 'real job' – at a global consulting firm – but my mother passed away just as I was meant to start. I began work four days after her funeral.

In 2018, I began to have symptoms of multiple sclerosis (MS) – although I didn't know it was MS at the time. I lost my sight in my right eye, and my ability to walk, but I was able to carry on working for quite some time, as my employer has a very flexible approach, so I could work from home and also make hospital appointments. My next job was with a UK asset-management company and it was there, while I was in my probationary period, that I was diagnosed with MS. They couldn't (then) offer the same level of flexibility, so it was a straight choice between my work and my health. I left and did manage to get the MS back into remission.

I found that I could work three days a week, but not full time – at least, not without quickly reaching burnout. I started looking for another job but knew it was like finding the proverbial needle in the haystack. But I then realised: this *shouldn't* be a needle in the haystack. There need to be more opportunities available to other people like me who want to continue to work or get back into the industry … but almost every role is being advertised as full time.

Disability is often looked at from the perspective of the people already in the workplace living with a disability … not from that of someone wanting to get into the industry or even moving from one post to another. It's also looked at purely in terms of capability rather than capacity. My problem – and that of many others – is capacity rather than capability. We can do an excellent job – just not five days a week.

With maternity leave and women returning, part-time working isn't totally alien to the industry and can be made to work in any job, so let's go one step further and make more jobs available part time. It won't just help people like myself: we've got some amazing candidates who currently aren't in the market because they aren't able to work full time for a variety of reasons. So now my career is trying to help people who, like myself, are going through some sort of stress-related problem.

I don't think it was a coincidence that my MS came on after a period of huge personal stress: over 50% of days off in the UK are caused by stress-related illnesses. And one of the factors I try and get employers to consider is the whole person. You have life stresses, such as your personal finances, as well as work stresses – and your ability to manage both effectively enables you to perform in your job and achieve your aspirations while maintaining a healthy life.

A lot of people don't actually speak up on what they are experiencing, which may be affecting their performance. Talking to – listening to – your employees is the first step to making the most of, and retaining, your single biggest asset: the people who work for you.

Leading change to ability equality

Katy Halliday, a director at a global asset manager, also previously led the Diversity Project's disability workstream. Here, she explains what her employer and the wider sector are doing to make progress towards ability equality.

Katy Halliday, Former Disability Workstream Leader

While I don't personally have a disability, I was offered the chance to help lead the Disability workstream because of my experience running employee networks, and I jumped at the chance.

I worked at BlackRock, where there's a really rich culture of employee-led networks right across the firm – from LGBT [lesbian, gay, bisexual and transgender] and Black through to women's and veterans' networks, even a Green Team. In 2016, disability and mental health networks didn't exist within BlackRock and I was asked to help set up the new network.

I met all the founders of the network, including a lady in the US who identified as having a disability and has had a fantastic career: a managing director and a real inspiration. She made me realise how awesome it would be to drive this issue forwards: people with disabilities have found themselves, for a long time, almost second-class citizens right across the world – not just in financial services. She brought it right to the surface for me and taught me why we should take the opportunity to make a stand and make a change.

I was heavily involved in the network for about eighteen months, serving as a global co-chair, and then BlackRock asked me to represent them at the Diversity Project. When the lady running the Disability workstream had to step down, I was asked to step in.

The Diversity Project now has a partnership with Scope to help drive the workstream forwards,[57] and we are looking at the whole of the employment lifecycle of a person with a disability: from talent attraction through to the interview process, the onboarding process, the first day in the office, and then development and talent retention. And we should break it down to understand the barriers at each stage, as well as add in people's personal stories and experiences, as that adds real power to the message.

For that, we decided that we needed experts to come in, to understand our business and our challenges, and present something back in bite-sized chunks... almost a best-practice guide that project members could reference and use. The bottom line was that we wanted to showcase the best-practice guidelines from the experts and ensure that all of our HR managers and our line managers really do understand some of the challenges that people with disabilities face. We also wanted to help them feel comfortable to get into conversations with people and ask what they were doing wrong, what they were doing right, what they could do better, and how they could help that individual.

How ahead or behind is the sector compared with other professions on dealing with this?

I don't think we're behind, particularly: the sector is on a journey, like other employers in the UK. It's where LGBT was ten years ago, gender twenty years ago. We're all trying to come up the curve together. I like to think that, because this is a well-trodden path, actually people are embracing it – they want to learn and educate themselves, rather than being frightened about it. It's a bumpy road to get there, but we've done it with other workstreams. I am hugely positive about this.

One of the challenges is that not all disabilities are immediately visible, so that can make it harder to get a message across and why we need to promote education with our line managers, HR managers, our colleagues as well…that what you see is not necessarily what you get. The drive for this needs to come both from within a company and from staff themselves. There are a number of reasons why employee networks are a good thing: as well as delivering change within an organisation, there are huge personal development opportunities. People telling their stories can also really help give it that extra punch.

It's also important for firms to recognise the total effect within the company and on people's perception of the business, talent recruitment and retention. I've worked with the summer interns for 2020, and they really embrace the work of employee networks – and almost expect it of a big company like BlackRock.

The Diversity Project approach

The Diversity Project is leading change in the sector through two workstreams, one focusing on disability and the other on neurodiversity. The leaders of these two projects, Tim Roberts and Meike Bliebenicht, share their experiences and explain what the project is doing to encourage change in the sector.

Tim Roberts, Disability Workstream Leader

I was born profoundly deaf, and work in a mostly mainstream environment. Generally speaking, my progress has been hindered by a lack of assistive technology and people's attitudes towards disability.

I work at an international bank in the Global Marketing team, so I have a lot of meetings with people from different countries, and that can be quite challenging – although I tend to find that many overseas people who can speak English tend to understand me better than those in the UK, and it's easier for me to understand too because they speak properly and don't abbreviate and use slang.

At times in my career, getting the right equipment – even a suitable tablet so that I can watch subtitles on one screen and do a presentation on another – has been a challenge, and has affected my performance. My employer has been great at providing a range of stuff for me, and I am thankful to work for such a great employer.

My other challenge has been awareness. If you have a disability, you have to do a lot more than just your job. Podcasts go out with no transcripts. When I have meetings, I have to book support (ie a captioner to type up what is being said on the call). If I have video meetings, I need more time between calls to prepare but not everyone understands that.

For those in a wheelchair, going to a meeting means planning your route, arranging support, taking more time to get there. Again, not everyone makes allowances, and they jam meetings together just because it suits them. My employer is working towards booking meetings for fifty minutes, because even though we are not in a big building, people do still need that time to go to the toilet, etc. That is a basic need, and disabled people may need a bit more time.

Other people will have issues around light or noise levels in an office that can make it difficult for them to perform. Many will simply not be able to get to an office during rush hour, need to take time out for medical appointments or find it problematic to work a full working week, just as a working parent might want slightly different hours around their children's school hours etc. This is why flexible working is so important.

If you want the talents of a particular person on your payroll, you need to find ways to make it possible. The recruitment process has changed quite a bit, but a lot of companies still have a long way to go on accommodating different types of disability. For instance, I'd obviously prefer a face-to-face meeting where I can lip read, rather than a telephone one; someone in a wheelchair may prefer a video or telephone call. Companies need to look at the forms people fill in when they say they have a disability and liaise with them on how best to conduct any interview. I've arrived at a company and they clearly haven't even registered the fact that I'm deaf, despite filling this in on the application form.

Oddly, smaller companies have been better at responding to issues like this because there is less red tape to cut through, while bigger companies aren't always good at sharing experiences and best practices between departments or even countries. In the Global Asset-Management division we have a Diversity and Inclusion Steerco to help identify areas of improvement and for people to share where things are working. No company is perfect, but I truly appreciate everything that my employer is doing for me.

It's not all negative. People's attitudes now are different to when I started my career. Twenty years ago, people didn't care. Now people are too politically correct and not sure what to do, so sometimes they take the easy way out – do nothing. The best managers I have worked for are the ones who tackle this head on and go, 'Right, this might be a challenge, but I like this person, I think they can do a good job for me and I will do everything I can to help them.'

In the big wide world out there, there's a long way to go, but the fact that the Diversity Project is being taken seriously shows that the will is there.

Meike Bliebenicht, Neurodiversity Workstream Leader

I have ADHD; and being the proud owner of a neurodivergent brain, I am thrilled by the benefits that neurodiversity will bring to our industry.

I'm currently Global Product Director at an asset-management firm and the word 'global' in my job title has meant a lot of travelling. It's also an arena where there is always a short-term volatility. This type of job really suits me. I love everything which is super-dynamic...getting to the office and thinking 'this is my to-do list'; then, after five minutes, everything is shuffled around. I thrive on short deadlines – anything which is highly energetic and dynamic. But I find it hard to deal with things that aren't like that – really to the extent where it freaks me out. Tasks which do not involve any activity on my side, such as having to read through piles of documents or listening to lectures, can actually make me quite anxious.

I always found that a bit odd. But while I have always had ADHD, I haven't always known it. What you are aware of from very early on is that, somehow, you're different. That can make you the outsider, because you struggle with things that others take for granted. Equally, certain things come to you very easily. For instance, I used to wonder why everybody else around me would get nervous before making a presentation to a large audience. To me, that's the quietest moment of my life. Why does nobody else feel that way?

But then, other people can quietly sit in a corner for hours and read research papers or microanalysis – something I struggle with. Especially hard for me is getting things into my head that I'm not particularly interested in: my brain is always trying to find more interesting things to do. I used to try and cover it up, because you can't turn up at a business meeting and say, 'Sorry, but that paper was unbelievably dull so I really couldn't get myself to read it.'

I don't like the word 'condition' when people talk about ADHD, autism and so on, because in the diversity context it's just a different way of being. It's not something wrong or something we need to cure, but you end up doing a lot of covering up because you don't want to stand out, especially not in a negative way. And because of that, rather like a duck swimming apparently effortlessly, beneath the surface there's an awful lot going on.

Doing all of that paddling just to appear 'normal' can be exhausting. You observe your peers and try to adopt their behaviours, all the time wondering why it's so hard for you. 'Everyone in this meeting is relaxed except for me – and I'm anxious about getting found out.' That's very common among those aged over thirty-five, because they likely didn't get a diagnosis as a kid. A lot of people actually get diagnosed because of something else: all of this covering up and additional work can affect your mental health. They are struggling with anxiety or depression, go to their GP and are referred to a psychiatrist, then discover there is something else triggering this.

For our industry, one of the biggest challenges is that neurodivergence is not always immediately obvious: you can't, for instance, see whether someone is dyslexic. High-functioning autism is similar. There can be distinct physical movements associated with autism, and avoidance of eye contact, but they're not severe enough for someone to say: 'There's something different about your brain.' They will just assume that you don't like small talk, and sometimes this is held against you as if you just don't care...or you don't have any 'team spirit'. ADHD is, at some point, visible. For instance, I use my hands a lot when I'm talking!

There seems to be some sort of unwritten rule that every person in the same job at the same level of seniority must have developed a similar skill set over time, and act and behave in a certain way. If you don't, this is often pointed out to you. In most cases, such feedback is well meant, but not accepting that there are many different ways of getting to the right result is one of the main obstacles to successful neuro-inclusion.

What are the advantages neurodivergent people can bring to the workplace?

Having a different perspective can help to challenge conventional ways of doing things. If someone's brain works differently, they solve problems differently. They may spot things that other people do not see.

Without falling into stereotypes, there are some very distinct skills which come with neurodiversity. Those with dyslexia, for example, often have very good people skills and a creative, entrepreneurial mindset. Autism can mean good problem-solving. Those with ADHD process information very quickly. Dyspraxia often goes with an ability to organise things and construct processes differently, and being very creative because of that.

In their 2018 report,[58] the CIPD reported that Microsoft, JPMorgan, EY, Google, SAP, DXC Technology, Ford and Amazon were all running neurodiversity-at-work initiatives, and that these pioneer organisations have demonstrated early successes. JPMorgan, for example, reports that 'after three to six months working in the Mortgage Banking Technology division, autistic workers were doing the work of people who took three years to ramp up – and were even 50% more productive'.[59]

Neither does employing neurodivergent staff necessarily mean major investment. The CIPD paper reports that: 'Employers surveyed by the US Job Accommodation Network found that as many as 59% of common adjustment types cost nothing for the employer. Technology, in particular assistive tech in the form of iPad apps such as speech-to-text software, is facilitating both the inclusion and performance optimisation of neurodivergent people such as non-verbal autistic people.'[60]

Within the investment industry itself, we are moving away from expecting the exact same skills profile or behaviour, but so far, these have been baby steps. It's going to take time. While having someone who is neurodivergent as part of a cognitively diverse team is an obvious asset, it is often questioned whether we necessarily make good people leaders: there is often a certain expectation of how senior leaders should behave and the skill set they should have acquired. Of course, there are good leaders with neurodiverse brains. Most neurodiverse brains are very authentic and extremely loyal. For me, these are two very important attributes of good leadership.

The bigger problem is whether you are able to progress beyond a certain level. A lot of those with neurodivergent brains will often have problems with something called 'executive functioning', which takes place in the prefrontal cortex. So, tasks such as planning, organising, modelling outcomes – while not impossible – can take a lot of energy. In particular, tasks related to organising and planning do not have to be a struggle; some help with admin can make a huge difference.

We still live in a world where struggles with these perceived 'simple' tasks are often interpreted as weaknesses or reduced ability. And being judged, and sometimes written off, like this might make it difficult for someone to really progress in higher levels of management.

This is a challenge which needs to be addressed urgently. From a business perspective, getting neurodivergent people in the right roles is critical. For instance, one of my first jobs was within a team called 'Strategy and Planning', where as far as I was concerned, nothing ever happened! I totally get that we need to do it, and that other people want to do it, but it just wasn't me. But then the financial crisis came along and suddenly we moved into firefighting crisis-management mode. It was at that point that it clicked: this is the type of job I need…something highly energetic, dynamic, immediate.

I don't need a crisis every day, but I do look to something which has a certain level of energy all the time, and I don't find that exhausting at all. It's what I'm naturally good at, what I need to do to survive.

The CIPD perspective on disability

The CIPD gives the following examples of adjustments that employers may make for disabled employees:[61]

- Make changes to premises such as automated doors or ramps.

- Review performance-management processes.

- Provide additional training to support employees to use new software.

- Introduce specialist equipment such as supportive chairs or height-adjustable desks.

- Review communication methods to support all staff requirements.

- Provide flexibility for time off for hospital appointments.

- Introduce flexible working.

The Diversity Project's perspective on neurodiversity

To attract neurodivergent candidates and fully benefit from the neurodiverse make-up of their workforce, investment management firms should consider the following:[62]

Recruiting neurodivergent talent

1. Simplify job descriptions. They should be concise, with clear distinctions between must-haves and nice-to-haves.

2. Demonstrate that neurodivergent talent is welcomed. Include case studies on recruitment websites or state your commitment to neurodiversity in job descriptions.

3. Post job vacancies on dedicated websites. For example, the charity Autism Speaks[63] runs an online jobs board, and the LinkedIn group The Spectrum Employment Community[64] is dedicated to employment for people on the autism spectrum.

4. Review your interview technique. Interviewers should be aware that neurodivergent candidates will often directly respond to the question asked and may not know how to expand in ways that will highlight their additional skills or experience. Training can help interviewers ask the right questions and interpret the responses they receive.

5. Provide direct feedback on interview performance. Many neurodivergent candidates struggle to 'read between the lines'. It will help them if your feedback is concise and to the point, especially if you decide not to take forward discussions.

Retaining neurodivergent talent

6. Educate your team. Neurodivergent colleagues often approach problems differently and come up with different solutions – sometimes quite radical ones. Without any knowledge of neurodiversity, there is a risk that such differences will be considered disruptive by other members of a team.

7. Tackle biases in the system. Ensure that neurodivergent individuals are not disadvantaged because they do not seem to be 'a good fit'. Biases need to be tackled not just in recruitment processes but also with career progression and performance measurement.

8. Allow for some accommodations. Simple changes can make a big difference; for example, not having to hot-desk, or being able to work from home one or two days a week.

Developing neurodivergent talent

9. Provide career support. Neurodivergent employees are often not aware of career opportunities, as they may struggle to understand

an organisation's structure or don't know how to network or what to say. Mentoring or coaching can help.

10. Provide leadership sponsorship. Leadership drives inclusion, so hiring, retention and promotion efforts will be more successful if senior management teams are aware of the benefits of neurodiversity and on board with your efforts to create a more inclusive workplace.

Five things to do

There is no 'one size fits all' approach to attracting and retaining people with disabilities – each person will have different needs and preferences – so it's important to consider all these things:

1. Make sure your recruitment processes are totally inclusive of disabled people: use images of people with disabilities on your website, welcome them in your job specs and ensure your interview processes work for them.

2. Give more time to people with disabilities to get to meetings or prepare for them. If someone needs additional resources – such as an interpreter or lipreader, or assistance getting to meetings – make those available.

3. Recognise that many disabled people would really benefit from flexible working – either more

home working or being part time – and may need to incorporate more medical appointments into their working week.

4. Coach and mentor your neurodivergent employees to utilise technology, employee networks and business practices to their advantage.

5. Talk to employees with a disability regularly to identify and iron out any problems that are arising. It might seem like a tricky subject to broach, and some managers are anxious about 'saying the wrong thing', but it's far better to be transparent and open than to do nothing.

FIVE

LGBT+

'I looked around me and saw people who weren't just LGBT but also from different ethnic backgrounds. And I thought: this is the generation coming through. By connecting them together there was a massive opportunity for the industry to effect change...not just in the LGBT world but in ethnicity and gender as well.'

— Colette Comerford, Diversity Project LGBT+ Workstream Leader[65]

Challenges and issues

The LGBTQ acronym is for lesbian, gay, bisexual, transgender and queer, although the 'Q' can also stand for questioning. You may also see LGBT+, LGBT*, LGBTx or LGBTQIA, where the I stands for intersex and A for asexual/agender. The A has also been used to refer to 'ally'. When considering LGBT+ it is important to understand the different terms and a full list can be found on the Stonewall website,[66] but for simplicity can be grouped into three themes:

1. Sexual orientation: how a person characterises their sexuality and includes terms such as gay, lesbian, bisexual and pansexual.

2. Gender identity and expression: how a person conceptualises themselves as male, female or neither, and includes terms such as transgender, cisgender, binary and genderqueer.

3. Attitudes: how a person's attitudes shape their views, and includes terms such as ally, sex positive, heterosexism, homophobia and transphobia.

LGBT employees comprise a significant portion of the workforce. The Office for National Statistics states that the proportion of the UK population identifying as lesbian, gay or bisexual increased from 1.5% in 2012 to 2.0% in 2017, and estimates that 1.1 million people aged 16 years and over identify as lesbian, gay or bisexual.[67]

Although perceptions of LGBT+ have become increasingly positive over recent years, there is still a stigma in some segments of society. A 2008 survey by the Williams Institute found that 38% of lesbian, gay or bisexual employees reported being harassed at work, and 27% experienced employment discrimination on the basis of their sexual orientation.[68] A 2010 survey found that 78% of transgender employees reported being harassed or mistreated at work, and 47% reported being discriminated against in terms of hiring, promotion or job retention.[69]

Lived experiences

I talked to Colette Comerford, Head of Inclusion and Culture and a leader of the Diversity Project's LGBT+ workstream, about her experiences. As Colette explains, people in the LGBT+ community may find it difficult to be open about their sexuality in the industry, partly because of the perception that doing so risks harming their career.

Colette Comerford, Diversity Project LGBT+ Workstream Leader

I'm Irish – I was born and grew up in a very small village. Even from the age of three or four, I just felt different. I had a lot of challenging conversations with my mum around what I wore and what I did: this is how I learned to negotiate at an early age!

The turning point was around the age of seven. I explicitly said in my letter to Santa that I did not want a doll. But I got one anyway and called it Boy George. I thought: if he can wear nail varnish and lipstick, why does my mum have a problem with me wearing jeans and a t-shirt and playing football?

The whole family laughed, and I sort of shut down at that point. Back then, nobody understood what I was thinking or feeling; I never said any of this. But my grandma said to me: 'Don't worry, Colette. You can call your doll whatever you want.' I went away from that point thinking: just always be yourself, stand up for what you believe in. My grandmother's always going to be there to support me.

I still have these challenges, but life just goes on.

As much as I loved my family, I knew I had to get away from this small town or close right down: escapism is quite a common theme in the LGBT+ community. Luckily, one of the people I played football with was a teacher, and she said that a local bank ran apprentice-type training. So off I headed to Dublin: the big city.

I left Dublin when I realised that it too was a very small place and I still had no one to talk to about what I was feeling and who shared my experiences. I then moved to London and worked for a UK bank where I had an incredibly immersive experience working with international clients. But all the time I was there, my work and weekend lives never crossed over.

In 2010 I ended up at an asset-management firm. The first week I was there, my manager took me for lunch with the rest of the team and asked me about myself and if I had a partner. In that split second when you're asked a question like that, you use your risk-assessing ability, and I thought: no one has ever asked me if I had a 'partner' – not 'boyfriend' or 'husband', but 'partner'. And I thought: I can actually say this now. After that, small talk in the office was, 'How was your weekend with your partner?' and that was a massive turning point for me. It had taken a lot for me to say it, but I felt I could… because of that one question.

The year before, I had my first experience of a contractor in my team experiencing homophobia, and she reported it to me. It was a really awful situation. It just didn't make any sense, but I had the support of my manager to help me through that. During conversations that followed about my personal development, my manager said to me, 'If you're going to lead your team, it's going to be about trust. How many of them know about you?' You let people in when you want to go bold. It's the starting point for innovation, change and transformation.

Leading change to LGBT+ equality

For the first four years of my career I worked closely with a colleague who became a friend. When he left to join another organisation, we met up for a beer, where he said, 'I need to tell you something. I always wanted to – but was too scared to say. I'm gay.'

I was really shocked. Not that he was gay, but that I'd always thought we had a really close relationship, and yet he had never felt able to share that important information with me. That was three decades ago, but in more recent times, another manager I'd worked with for ten years told me he was getting married to his male partner – and that was the first conversation we'd had about him being gay.

I've always tried to be open in relationships with everyone I've worked with, but in both those scenarios, people I thought I'd been fairly close to had chosen not to share something quite significant with me. I was thinking, what was it about my behaviour that stopped that conversation from happening sooner? My conclusion was that my colleagues were on their own journey and I had no idea of the challenges they might have faced in the workplace.

In my current role as chief executive at Punter Southall Aspire, I feel it is important that I take lead in creating a welcoming workplace and have become an LGBT Great role model and ally, publicising this step on the company website and in news articles.[70] This provides a clear message to future and current employees, clients and stakeholders that this is an important issue to me and the business. The company is not large enough to create our own LGBT networks, so we have leaned on the Diversity Project for events, webinars and reports that provide learning and support for all our staff. There is still much more we can do as we continue on our journey; having created the space and culture for conversations to take place, we need to allow the culture to develop organically.

The Diversity Project approach

Raising awareness of LGBT+ challenges among the wider workforce is the focus of the Diversity Project's LGBT+ workstream, which is comprised of an umbrella group made up of LGBT Great,[71] InterInvest[72] and the Investment Association.[73]

The workstream has the following two goals:

1. To develop LGBT+ diversity and inclusion across the industry
2. To identify and promote best practices to support LGBT+ people and allies

Colette Comerford and Matt Cameron, who are leading the workstream together, share some of the challenges they have faced at work and what managers can do to improve the situation.

Colette Comerford and Matt Cameron, LGBT+ Workstream Leaders

Matt: As a gay man, I was very much part of a minority group where I was brought up in a small northern town: until I went to university, I didn't know any other LGBT people. After uni, I moved to London, not knowing what I wanted to do, and found it very difficult to access any of the big firms. I didn't have any contacts, and while I had a 2:1 from a red-brick university, I didn't have one from Oxbridge.

I ended up in investment recruiting, and in the five years that I was there we expanded from 8 to 120 people. I exited in 2015 to set up my own diversity and inclusion recruitment business, The Ocean Partnership, joining forces with my co-MD Clare Scott, who had a similar background to mine. As well as recruitment and consultancy research, we moved increasingly into diversity and inclusion advisory – and that's why I started getting involved with the Diversity Project in 2016.

We ran some research looking at the barriers in terms of the LGBT+ agenda within the industry, and that's when we decided to develop a role-modelling programme called Project 1000.[74] We gained so much momentum that firms asked us to talk to them about the agenda, and we started to think about developing Project 1000 into a strategic offering. That became LGBT Great, which we launched in January 2019 with five founding members. Membership is helping us to fund programmes and, as of today, we have thirty members – globally.

Colette: My manager knew from feedback that some people at work wanted to start an LGBT network and suggested I run it. I had no experience of creating a network, but thought that if I didn't do it, who would?

That first day, I went down the corridor to meet the others who were interested in being in a network and almost turned around through anxiety about who was going to be in the room. But guess what? They were all people I knew…and we just found each other. When you meet someone like you in the industry, it's like you've found a friend – because you both know where you're coming from.

In 2016 I joined the Diversity Project, and one of the first conversations was with Matt – who had been a great supplier to us at Ocean, helping us to think about inclusion and diversity. After a few months I thought that Matt might be gay, but I didn't really know.

So, as we sat round the table at the Diversity Project, I wondered: if I mention my partner's name, would Helena or anyone around the table ever talk to me again? Because you always have that fear – will this affect my career and my relationships with people? You just carry that with you. But Matt spoke up to say he'd be happy to lead on LGBT – and it took off from there.

I looked around me and saw people who weren't just LGBT but also from different ethnic backgrounds. And I thought: this is the generation coming through. By connecting them together, there was a massive opportunity for the industry to effect change – not just in the LGBT+ world but in ethnicity and gender as well. That was the build-up to LGBT Great's launch – and since then it has been incredible.

Do either of you still experience homophobia within the industry?

Matt: Not necessarily direct attacks or homophobia. What we do experience is 'micro aggressions', where people say, 'I know someone gay like you,' or 'I've got a gay cousin,' or 'That's so gay.' It's basically a lack of understanding around the impact of language, but does (usually) demonstrate positive intent. It's a case of not knowing how to have the conversation.

Colette: Some use phrases like that because it was OK at school and they haven't moved on or realised it's not OK to say it now.

Matt: We've got over five hundred role models now, and in total I've probably heard only twenty or thirty horrendous experiences from industry employees – some where employees have just had to leave. But they're few and far between, and I don't think it's a particular reflection of our industry, because I know this happens in other sectors too.

Colette: Our role is to send out a strong signal, to help the environment change and bring it into the modern world; otherwise, we won't attract and retain people. The generation coming through are from environments where their friends are gay; there's sex education in school on LGBT+ and gender fluidity. And they are looking for employers because they are looking for equality in all its forms and what it stands for.

Young people are speaking up and standing up for each other; lots of staff are learning through their children. So, there's a massive opportunity to connect with that. They're also conscious through the stories we share – about how we've been affected and felt vulnerable. They don't want their own child to be struggling like that. They want an open conversation about what's going on in their mind and want to know how they can help them.

How much progress are you making?

Matt: What I see in the industry is that, while support for LGBT+ is not necessarily open or visible, when you actually ask the question, the people who you least think will be supportive actually are. Even in places like Republican parts of the States, execs will tell you that while they've been brought up not to embrace LGBT+ equality, they know they have a duty or an obligation to accept and to help everybody regardless, and they tell you what they've been doing to help LGBT+ colleagues. It's about acceptance of differences, regardless of if we agree.

Colette: Now gay and lesbian couples in their thirties have got married, had kids, so there's a change in the narrative from how things were when we started. They're breaking barriers in so many ways – and they're role models for the generation coming through. We're not just talking about gay men or women, but bisexuality too. And you're finding out the backgrounds and different challenges that each of them have – in places like New York, Hong Kong, Singapore, India. To step forward now is incredible: it feels like it has just ignited this whole LGBT+

subject, and shone a light on the people who already existed... but nobody knew that important part of them.

What should middle managers be thinking about in terms of managing their teams? How should they be modifying their behaviour? And what behaviours should they be encouraging within their team?

Colette: The role of the 'manager' has moved on from just managing performance and deliverables. You have to move away from focusing on the technical and focus on your people.

Managers need to connect with their people and understand their personal values: what drives them in terms of behaviours, and how that aligns with company culture. Even that one signal to me from my manager using neutral language enabled me to open up. Get to know your people, their strengths. You'll get a lot more out of people if you explore their minds and get to the bottom of the things they do outside work.

What's more, clients are asking us more and more about the diversity of our teams. How do you make decisions? How do you avoid groupthink, apply better judgement? How do you show 'difference'? What are you doing to increase workforce diversity? The pressure is now on managers who have to turn this corner, because otherwise it will affect how you win, do and retain business.

Matt: It all has to come down to inclusive management, leadership style and a team culture of equality. A team which is multigenerational, intersectional and making it easy: breaking things down into actions that help team members experience empathy for others, and including everyone in key decision-making. The middle manager has to lead by being the role model within the team who sets the right values and tone.

Vicarious reinforcement means that others will naturally follow and copy the leader if they are praised. We talk about allyship a lot as well. Not just in the context of LGBT+. It's important that it's broader than that. We constantly talk about the 'five traits of impactful allyship': self-discovery, empathy, courage, responsibility and persistence.

Colette: Managers can look at the whole team, but you have to break it down and have a relationship with an individual. We never know what might have gone on in that person's life to make them feel vulnerable. I've had LGBT friends who haven't told me, but something may have happened to make them feel vulnerable and we need to break that down. Share your own experiences, show some of your own vulnerabilities, and hopefully that will open things up.

Matt: People will sometimes not have the conversation for fear of not knowing what language to use and getting it wrong. It's absolutely OK not to know the ins and outs of language, and it's fine to get it wrong. Again, it's got to be role-modelled from leadership: to create a space where you can have those conversations, and sometimes get it wrong, and know how to apologise. Generally, if you give that opportunity, people will embrace it.

Colette: One of the challenges is that LGBT+ has followed the same route as BAME – Black, Asian and other minority ethnic groups – with everything chucked into one acronym. We all have our unique differences – and challenges! For instance, there's a lot of biphobia, even within the LGBT community, and trans, non-binary identities are so far behind – so we as a community have to do a lot more on language ourselves.

What would progress look like a couple of years from now?

Matt: Our target is 1,000 individual role models, and we're halfway there now. We aim to show how they are helping to inspire and motivate others through their stories. We're one of the most energised workstreams, and role-modelling is part of that.

Colette: You can't achieve anything unless everyone shares accountability, so, for me, progress would be everybody getting involved in some way from a diversity and inclusion perspective. One of the challenges about being a role model and being visible is that you are constantly coming out, all the time, and a huge amount of energy goes into it. That's why we need this solidarity so that no one feels like they're carrying the flag alone.

Young people will come through as the narrative is changing and say: the problem is not us, it's you. So, we as organisations have to fix ourselves right now. If we want people with all of these values and strengths, then why would we blind-CV them, assess them the same way or take away their identity to fit in with us?

The CIPD perspective

Communication and training

- Promote the organisation's commitment to LGBT+ inclusion.

- Educate staff about their personal responsibility to treat colleagues with respect, highlighting a zero-tolerance approach to bullying, harassment and discrimination.

- Train staff about how to report bullying, harassment or discrimination on the basis of sexual orientation or gender identity.

- Set objectives for line managers to promote inclusion and support trans and LGBT+ staff.

- Establish LGBT+ employee networks within the organisation and work together to promote the importance of diversity and inclusion across the organisation.

Reviewing employment practices

- Appoint senior executives with responsibility for diversity issues, including a sponsor for LGBT+ inclusion.

- Review recruitment and selection processes so there are no sexual orientation or gender identity biases.

- Include a diversity statement in all job advertisements.

- Develop and promote performance-management processes, career paths and promotional opportunities for all.

- Review conditions of employment to ensure fairness and legal compliance.

- Ensure the language/written words used across the business is gender-neutral.

- Have policies on transitioning at work, diversity, equal opportunities and anti-bullying.[75]

Five things to do

1. If your company doesn't already have one, set up an LGBT+ network.

2. Encourage those who are happy to come forward to share their stories and act as champions.

3. Reinforce that your company is LGBT+ friendly, and that employees are welcome to talk to you about any issues they face.

4. Emphasise your LGBT+ stance in your recruitment materials.

5. If you feel there are negative attitudes that need to be addressed in the company, organise some training on unconscious bias.

SIX

Smart Working

'The demand in flexibility of location, working hours and contractual flexibility is higher than ever, and we predict this trend will only continue to grow. For organisations to retain and attract the best and most diverse talent it's important to view effective and sustainable SMART Working as a powerful tool to Build Back Better.'

— Ana Maria Tuliak – Chair of the Diversity Project SMART Working Workstream[76]

Challenges and issues

In Chapter Three I shared my own perspective on flexible working, describing how my new employer's intransigence over working from home several days a week led to me leaving and setting up my own business. To me, there was no choice. Playing a key role in my children's early years was more important than remaining on my career trajectory.

This was some twenty years ago: a time when many women, but relatively few men, were having that decision forced upon them. I was fortunate: while it might have slowed my career progress, it didn't halt it. Countless talented people have been lost to the industry because their bosses assumed that if they couldn't see you at your desk working, you must be skiving.

The last few years have marked a sea change in companies' attitudes towards employees electing to work part time, to work away from the office, to job share or to compress their hours into fewer days. 'Presenteeism' hasn't gone away, but it is definitely receding into the distance. The Covid-19 pandemic has turbo-boosted this shift: we now know that people can be trusted to work from home. The streets, offices and coffee bars in the City of London might have been deserted for months, but the sector continued serving its clients, customers and shareholders. The sky hasn't fallen down.

This section looks beyond flexible working to explore a raft of other practices that come under the heading of 'smart working'. In particular, it looks at how smart working is the biggest single factor that enables a business to recruit and retain people from a more diverse talent pool.

What is smart working?

The terms 'smart working' and 'flexible working' tend to be used interchangeably. They are both broadly used to describe work patterns that allow employees to achieve a better work/life balance, while making it easier for employers to attract and retain talent that might otherwise be unavailable to them.

In many cases, flexible working is what makes it possible for a person to work at all, because of other demands, such as caring responsibilities, access issues or health considerations. Smart working is central to all the workstreams of the Diversity Project simply because it enables so many people who would otherwise be excluded from our sector to bring their talents to the industry and maximise their personal and professional potential.

When designing a flexible role, it's important to consider where, when and how the work will be done. The term can describe any kind of work pattern that doesn't fit into the traditional nine-to-five, five-day week based in the employer's workplace. Examples include:

- Flexitime

- Part time

- Working from home for part or all of the week

- Annualised hours (when employees work a set number of hours over a year, fluctuating from week to week or month to month)

- Compressing the working week into fewer days

Having people in the office for fewer days of the week opens up the opportunity to reshape the working environment to incorporate co-working or hot-desking, reduce head office presence and increase regional presence, or adopt solutions such as 'core and flex' where a business permanently occupies a fixed amount of space in a building and hires extra space as and when it is needed.

The technology required to work and meet remotely has been in place for some time, but the experience of Covid-19 has made everyone far more attuned to holding virtual meetings – often avoiding the time and expense involved in gathering staff in one place. At the start of the first lockdown, businesses worked minor miracles to enable staff to work and access sensitive company data from home.

Because of smart working's pivotal role, in 2019 the Diversity Project and Timewise launched a collaborative effort to modernise working practices in the investment and savings industry. The aim was to deepen understanding around the cultural and operational barriers to flexible working in more roles, identify specific actions to overcome these barriers, and test and share solutions. The programme is supported by AXA Investment Managers, Aon, Fidelity International and St James's Place Wealth Management. At the time of writing, the core partners are starting to implement recommendations with support from the Diversity Project and Timewise.

Critically, the Diversity Project and its partner Timewise assert that flexible roles should be quality, permanent ones that benefit employers and employees alike, so they do not include zero-hours or temping contracts.

What the law says

At present, even if you don't have flexible working written into your HR policies as standard, all employees can ask for it as individuals. That right was established in 2014 under the Flexible Working Regulations.

There are some caveats: the employee must have been working for the same employer for at least twenty-six weeks, their request must be made in writing, and they can only make the request once a year. What's more, when they submit their application, the employee has to set out what effect they think it would have on the business. You, as an employer, are entitled to say 'no' – but you are legally obliged to deal with any request 'in a reasonable manner'. This means properly considering the request, meeting the employee to discuss it and giving them the option to appeal if you turn their request down.

That's the default legal position: it's primarily reactive and places the onus on the employee. Even with the legal right available to them, many employees in the investment and savings sector have shied away from asking for flexibility because of the perception that it would either not be granted or be seen as displaying a lack of loyalty or ambition.

Many companies' HR policies on flexible working do, in fact, go further than the statutory minimum obligations, but a common problem is that many employees, even managers, aren't familiar with these policies. The alternative is to develop a company-wide HR strategy around flexibility that lets everyone know where they stand and acts as the starting point for developing ways of working that make the most of the potential benefits of smart working – and boosts the company's ability to attract and retain talent.

The impact of Covid-19

The focus on flexible working has been amplified by Covid-19. Across the globe, investment and savings firms have been forced – at pace and under pressure – to revise long-standing working practices and embrace remote working.

In the words of Helena Morrissey, Chair of the Diversity Project:

'The real-life experience has demonstrated what was hard to prove in theory: that people can be at least as productive working from home as in the office and that almost every job in our industry can be performed remotely.

'It's broken the stigma attached to remote
working in one fell swoop. Culturally, we had
struggled to move away from "presenteeism" –
where hours at the (same) desk were viewed
as a measure of commitment and performance.
Now it's all about results. If we can build
on these learnings, this is potentially a huge
equaliser for men and women and a magnet
for diverse talent.'[77]

As this book goes to press, business leaders across the
globe are starting to realise that the initial response to
implementing remote working needs to be developed
more strategically to make it a longer-term means of
harnessing talent. Equally importantly, it has opened
the door to considering other types of flexible working,
such as different working hours. For the investment
industry, which has often struggled to modernise its
working practices, this is an opportunity to improve
employee engagement and performance, attract
diverse talent through new ways of working, and drive
efficiencies and cost savings on office space.

The point about cost savings is significant. In an article
in the *Financial Times* on 3 January 2021, Daniel Thomas
quoted a Savills report that office vacancies had risen
from 5.5% to 6.5% in 2020.[78] He mentioned that companies are already reconsidering how much office space
they need: 'Many companies plan to downsize, cut
costs and push through permanent hybrid models of
working between the office and the home.' With staff

at so many levels able to work from home, more companies are intending to use 'hub-and-spoke' models, where the head office is the 'corporate showroom' and more use is made of regional offices.

In the wake of what my own company has learned during the pandemic, we estimate we can significantly reduce our property costs without affecting performance.

Supporting statistics

The statistics show that when making decisions about staying in a job or looking for a new one, many talented people favour companies that offer flexible ways of working:

- 84% of men, 91% of women and 92% of Millennials either work flexibly or wish they could.[79]

- 15% of current vacancies reference flexible working at the point of hire.[80]

- Flexible working is considered highly important or essential for 77% of women, 80% of people with health concerns, 91% of carers and 74% of older workers.[81]

- 68% of organisations are taking steps to reduce stress and improve wellbeing in the workplace, and 69% of those organisations are using flexible working to achieve this.[82]

- 63% of employees are more likely to stay with an employer who offers flexible working.[83]

- It costs an average of £30,000 to replace an employee.[84]

- Nine in ten employees consider flexible working to be a key motivator to their productivity at work, and 81% of those who have access to remote working believe it increases their productivity.[85]

- In highly flexible working environments, only 2% more Millennial workers than workers from other generations see themselves leaving their job within two years, rather than staying beyond five; in the least flexible organisations, the gap widens to 18%.[86]

Leading change to smart working

My own company has been making changes to give more flexibility to employees and managers so they can manage their work/life balance.

First of all, we consulted all employees about what might work best for them. Importantly, we discovered that some employees wanted to swap salary for flexibility to achieve a better work/life balance. This goes to show that managers need not assume that they will be on the 'losing' end of any compromises.

We then introduced the flexible working arrangements that would benefit the company and employees, as I describe in the next section.

Smart working arrangements

We now offer a range of flexible working options to employees.

Flexitime

With this option, the employee is free to set their own work hours each day, within business limits and with the agreement of their manager. There are three components to flexitime:

- **Core period:** the hours in a workday when all staff are needed. At my company, the core period is from 9.30am to 12pm and 2pm to 4pm, which is when meetings are most likely to be scheduled and customer contact is heaviest.

- **Bandwidth:** the hours during which managers allow flexible scheduling in the office. It defines the earliest time employees may arrive and the latest time they may leave. At my company, these times are 8am and 6.30pm.

- **Flexible hours:** the hours an employee chooses to work. Employees can adjust their work schedules from day to day without getting approval first, as long as they complete their full working week.

Compressed working week

This is a flexible schedule where an employee does a full working week in fewer than five days by working more hours each day. The most common example is a four-day week (nine or more hours a day).

Five-day week plus four-day week

Under this option, an employee works for nine days over a two-week period.

Part-time working

This is when an employee works a reduced working week. It includes anything from working one day a week to four days a week, and the days worked can be fixed or changed each week.

Working from home

We consider any employee's request to work from home, although it is more suitable for some roles than others. Jobs that involve project work or an identifiable output often lend themselves to being managed from home, but in some instances, an employee working from home can have a negative impact on their colleagues.

Career breaks and sabbaticals

We provide the option of a career break or sabbatical so employees can refresh themselves and re-examine their priorities, get a 'second wind' before the next stage of their career, or prioritise something or someone else for a few months: an ailing relative, a struggling relationship, a partner's career, or health. Our midlife reviews, covered in Chapter Three, often lead to a conversation around older staff taking an extended break.

Our sector has traditionally interpreted taking a sabbatical as a lack of ambition, but I have seen in my own business that six months away from the front line can put fresh wind in someone's sails, forestalling an early retirement. Although we don't want to lose a valued member of staff, we consider one employee's sabbatical as an opportunity to test out our 'rising stars', and there are always plenty of highly qualified people keen to take on an interim role.

To show we are genuinely open to the concept, rather than simply paying it lip service, we let employees know it's an option we'd consider, rather than hiding it away in our terms and conditions of service.

The benefits

These arrangements have led to the following benefits in my company:

- It makes better use of our employees' time and energy. They spend less time commuting, or do so outside peak hours.

- It has increased the pool of qualified job applicants keen to work for us.

- It has helped us retain valuable employees by allowing them to adjust their hours to meet personal needs instead of having to use their leave or resign.

- There is less use of paid leave. Employees have more time to schedule personal matters during non-work hours, or they can more easily make up the time.

- We can organise our work better. Periods of peak activity and idle time are better managed so we can do more work in the same number of hours.

- If an employee is late, they can make up their time at some other point during the week.

- We're more efficient. Employees can set their own start times to suit their biological clocks, so we can take advantage of their most productive hours.

- We're more productive. We now measure performance purely on results or contributions – not on time spent in the office.

- Time is scheduled more effectively. Meetings, visits and phone calls can be scheduled during core hours, creating more 'quiet' time for work requiring concentration.

- Morale is higher. Employees have more control over part of their work environment, so they are more satisfied with their work.

Lived experience

Taken from our internal company-wide panel discussion to promote inclusion and diversity, one of our older employer benefit consultants describes his experience in flexible working over recent years.

Employee Benefit Consultant

It was in 2015 that I last worked a conventional nine-to-five, five days a week out of the Bristol office as an employee benefit consultant. We had around forty people in an open plan office space, which meant a number of distractions throughout the day, and so I started to work from home periodically just to get things done with some peace and quiet.

What I discovered was that the role did not depend on me being in the office all the time. In fact, once a week to talk stuff through face to face and focus on the business plan was generally enough.

In 2016 I changed my work pattern to Monday, Tuesday and Thursdays, based mainly from home and sometimes in the office. This gave me extra time to do other activities in the week such as project managing a barn conversion and making new friends while working for St Peter's Hospice, a charity that provides end-of-life care in the Greater Bristol area. The change has been very rewarding and the flexibility has meant that I have continued to work rather than leave the workplace in order to do all the things I want to do at this time in my life.

The Diversity Project approach

Given that smart working is so beneficial for diversity and inclusion, the Diversity Project has been leading the charge on making it the default practice in the investment and savings industry. Together with Timewise, a dedicated workstream has developed the *Manifesto for Change* for members of the Diversity Project. The manifesto outlines a series of actions for employers to take, supported by a practical framework.

Their agenda for change looks like this:

1. Leaders must champion flexible working to set the vision of the organisation.

2. Flexible working arrangements will be reason-neutral.

3. Flexibility will be designed into jobs as standard.

4. Managers will be supported to build their capabilities to manage flexible and dispersed teams.

5. Managers should take a proactive approach to reviewing flexible working arrangements. I talked to two of the key people driving this agenda: Ana Maria Tuliak, Executive Recruiter and workstream leader from the Diversity Project, and Emma Stewart from its partner, Timewise. They described the progress they are making – and how Covid-19 may influence this in years to come.

Ana Maria Tuliak, Diversity Project Smart Working Workstream Leader

I've worked with clients within the investments and savings industry for the last decade, and during that time I've seen the diversity and inclusion agenda steadily advance as the benefits within firms become more apparent. Slowly but surely, there's been a growing realisation that smart working is at the heart of making this happen – not just as an enabler for making workplaces more inclusive, but also making them more productive and more attractive.

Flexibility has traditionally been seen as a benefit for those who have served time or achieved seniority – not as a way to attract and retain the top diverse talent. Now it is.

In part, that shift has been driven by market dynamics. After the last recession, complacency among employers in our industry was quite high. Employees, especially graduates, were happy just to have a job. As the market has recovered, diversity and inclusion have risen up the agenda. 'What works for the employee' has been talked about more openly, as this is the key factor in (to apply a commonly used phrase in this context) 'inviting people not just to come to the party, but to join in the dancing'.

Covid-19 has massively accelerated that trend. Before then, in my experience, the majority of investment firms still highly valued presenteeism: being seen at your desk, the way it had always been done. Now managers are having to change their metrics, and the world after Covid-19 will simply not be the same as the one before the lockdown.

The way remote working has been shown to work will give people throughout an organisation more confidence to ask for this, and other forms of flexible working, from both their current employer and any future one. In fact, in a survey we carried out during the pandemic with over 500 participants in the investments and savings industry taking part, 66% of respondents agreed that they didn't see the workplace as their primary work location in the future.[87] Confidence to ask really is a key issue here, as I know from my own experience. Having worked for six and a half years in the industry, and not feeling able to ask for more flexibility, I took a six-month sabbatical. When I came back, I reprioritised my life and I felt able to assert that I would be more productive if I could work from home on Mondays to get on top of my strategy and plans for the week ahead. I have been working flexibly, location- and hours-wise, ever since! Through the Diversity Project and my network of executives and leaders within the industry, I and others have been lobbying firms to focus on outcomes as the main measure of productivity, rather than how many hours you've put in at the office. Yes, being in the office is important for collaboration, building relationships and creativity, but it's not the only measure of performance, just because it's a habitual cultural behaviour within organisations and has been for so many years.

The research undertaken by Timewise, pre Covid-19, has in fact shown that 87% of jobseekers in the UK are expecting some sort of flexibility,[88] and this has been very visible with the candidates I work with. However, I see so many examples of there still being a disconnect between what employees want and what some employers are prepared to provide. Just before Covid-19, we were talking to an organisation whose perceived 'flexibility' was to allow line managers to decide whether someone who asked could work from home for half a day a week – but only if they had a good reason, such as needing to be in to get their boiler fixed. This is a highly reactive, rather than proactive approach: offering flexibility should be reason-neutral, and part of your organisational culture – not a 'benefit' within a manager's gift.

Another candidate came to us after they lost a parent: a challenging time for anyone. Even though their employer had a policy in place to support flexible working, they wouldn't support that person to work flexibly to support their circumstances. They were so focused on presenteeism that it eventually led to a parting of ways. Another candidate left their employer because – even though their employer was well aware that they were neurodivergent – they couldn't provide the flexibility for them to attend hospital appointments.

How difficult will employers find it to switch from valuing presenteeism to quantifying outcomes?

Some will find it difficult because it's quite a big change in mentality, not just in working practices. Having said that, as we are passing one year milestone from the first lockdown (and we are still effectively living the 'forced working from home experiment'), we predict that the shift to sustainable flexible working practice should be smoother for firms which consciously and strategically committed to this culture change. 'Hybrid working as a standard' should be inevitable as we exit the government-imposed lockdown restrictions. Our experience shows that the firms that have done well with this have already been on a journey embedding flexibility within their core values before Covid-19 or have been fast to seize this crisis to bring their managers on board to understand, appreciate and support them in implementing flexible working practice for the long run.

Conversely, many companies will tell you that they already have flexible working enshrined in their company policies, but the reality is somewhat different. I know of one company which had a flexible working policy in place for over twenty years, but no one had ever worked flexibly for them. The prevailing culture of presenteeism hadn't supported it, and everyone had been too scared to do it first because of that.

Within that firm, it was only after one of their star fund managers role-modelled working out of the office that it slowly began to gain acceptance – starting with more senior personnel – but a lot of communication had to be done internally to get to the point where the culture came across as acceptable and supportive of this.

It has to come from the top: all too often you have groupthink within the boardroom, and they then don't support the middle and line managers. Managers must have the right training support and the right tools to create and nurture a flexible working environment.

How are you raising awareness of the business case?

At a SMART Working webinar held in June discussing ways to boost flexible working in the industry, Nick Miller, Head of Asset Management Department – Wholesale Supervision at the FCA talked about the un-diverse nature of our sector: 'One of the barriers that has prevented more women, more diverse candidates, going into these roles is the perception that the hours are incredibly long, you've got to be in the office from the crack of dawn through to quite late in the evening [...]. That doesn't help for childcare responsibilities, caring responsibilities and it's been proven we don't need to operate like that, we can operate in a more flexible way.' The FCA announced in January that it would look at diversity as part of its assessments of culture at firms and expected asset managers to put in place measures to promote inclusivity. It said diversity and inclusion 'underpinned' good culture.

Fortunately, there's been plenty of conversations and research published to demonstrate that without flexible working, as an employer you won't be able to attract and retain a diverse workforce, affecting your business prospects long term. What's more, as well as bullet-proofing your business for the future, you are working on your environmental, social and governance (ESG), acting in the interests of the broader stakeholders of society. Firms also need to be aware that generational forces will also soon start to shift the argument, as more Millennials enter the boardroom, and the old ways of thinking are replaced, and the barriers overcome.

Remote working is still currently enforced, but the mission is far from complete. While companies of every size are struggling with the impact of the pandemic, hard-won gains in diversity and inclusion are at risk. Economists, politicians and business leaders agree that the crisis will have an uneven economic impact, with minorities and women among the hardest hit. So, as we experiment with the new ways of working, leaders have the opportunity to rewrite the playbook on inclusive work practices further than they ever imagined.

What other arguments need to be won?

Before Covid-19 'the go to excuse' by a number of investment managers was along the lines of 'Oh, we'd love to try it, but the regulator doesn't allow it. Fund managers cannot work remotely.' There was contention that fund managers working out of another location present an increased risk of insider trading. This is indeed a myth, but it has persisted for a while and acted as a major deterrent. In reality many fund managers have been working flexibly, and functioned very well. And I would be very surprised if this myth doesn't stay just a myth as we come out of this pandemic, as we now have a yearlong proof/track record. To support this, the speech by Nikhil Rathi, CEO of the Financial Conduct Authority, at the launch of the HM Treasury Women in Finance Charter Annual Review this March was hugely encouraging as he acknowledged that diversity will be crucial in their consideration of vulnerability, particularly as we come out of a pandemic that has disproportionately affected women and people of colour: 'As part of our regulatory work on diversity and inclusion and the listings framework, we will be exploring whether we should make diversity requirements part of our premium listing rules.'[89]

And while the regulator seems to be heading in the right direction, latest research by Timewise confirms there is still a lot of work to be done.[90] Their flexible working index for 2020 shows that the demand for flexible working still hugely outstrips the supply across the UK – 8% of jobs are advertised as part time (and only 22% advertised with any flex at all). This raises a lot of questions. In fact, a lot of employers say to me: 'We'll be flexible for the right person.' But when they come to choose between two candidates, they'll go with the safe option (a person that conforms to the 9am–5pm working from the office) because that is what they know. Part of my work is to challenge these old ways of working and thinking, and to let employers clearly understand that the top talent now requires flexible working as a standard.

The final hurdle is the UK government giving employees the legal right to work from home, which we have seen some of our European counterparts, such as Finland and Germany, implementing in 2020.[91] For example, the Finnish 'Working Hours Act' will give the majority of full-time employees the right to decide when and where they work for at least half of their working hours.[92]

Until then, the onus continues being on employers and it is crucial now, more than ever, for industry leaders to adapt a more sustainable approach to flexible working. The choices we make now will inevitably affect performance during the recovery and beyond. Flexible working can and absolutely should be the new norm.

Emma Stewart, Chief Executive, Timewise

My own life experience and the barriers I met in my career have gone into Timewise: I set the business up in 2005 because I fell out of work as a senior TV producer after having children. I'd describe Timewise as a social business with a mission to get everybody the flexibility they need in the workplace without compromising their careers.

Timewise undertakes a lot of research, thought leadership and campaign work to champion the benefits of flexibility, and provides consultancy and training for employers who want to get better at flexible working. We also run our own job site for candidates who are returning to work, or who have negotiated more flexibility in the job they're in and can't find any jobs to apply for that will give them the same flexibility.

How much of a problem is flexible working for the industry?

We run a national index each year tracking the vacancy market, and only 15% of job advertisements mention any form of flexibility[93] – so 85% of six million job vacancies say nothing at all about an organisation's openness to have a conversation about flexibility. Yet research carried out in 2020 shows that, following Covid-19, nine out of ten people in the workforce now want to work flexibly.[94]

Many people are now working flexibly because they have negotiated it from their employer, and, of course, they want it in their next job. So, what happens? They look at job ads that don't mention flexibility and don't apply for them. Or there's a 'game of chicken' when they apply and wonder when to ask about it: when they apply, in the interview or after they are offered the job? The onus is all on the candidate.

The bottom line is that there are really good people who won't be applying for certain jobs because they are not confident enough to have that conversation.

How does the sector compare in its approach to flexibility?

While there has been some openness to flexible working, there hasn't really been that much good practice in the context of advertising jobs as flexible at the point of hire. And when you get into a conversation around management practice and capability, it maybe hasn't gone so deep as some of the other professional service firms.

Internationally, if you look west we compare relatively favourably with the States, where we know there are still some real challenges, especially related to workers' rights.

If we look to Europe there are some really interesting lessons that we can learn, particularly from the Scandinavian countries, where people are encouraged to balance work and care more effectively. We probably sit between the two.

For instance, only 7% of workers in our sector work part time (compared to a UK average of 28%).[95] This was why in 2020, the Diversity Project and Timewise launched a joint project with support from four founding partners to dig under the skin of why there are barriers to improving flexible working within the industry, and to try and understand what are the constraints: are they operationally real or simply perceived because of fixed mindsets and company cultures?

Our main concern is that it's currently all very reactive. Individuals at a senior level are able to negotiate and get what they want because they are very highly valued. Those new to the industry or in more junior roles don't feel they can necessarily ask – certainly not without impacting on their career progression. So, there's a non-conversation happening.

There are a number of risks that we see, which affects people in different ways and predominantly affects women more. You ask to go part time, and the employer says yes – but the job isn't really redesigned to reflect that. You're still expected to produce the same outputs. The answer to that is to support managers to redesign jobs differently if someone goes part time, as well as work out how to get the additional output out of somebody else.

'Returners' present another cause for concern. They leave because they can't balance work and care, so the best way to attract them back into organisations should be to give them the flexibility they need. Businesses keen to attract returners will set up returner programmes focused around coaching and getting people back up to speed. But all too often the job itself isn't flexible; or, if it is, they haven't redesigned the outputs and expectations for it being part time.

What, then, is the solution?

A far more effective solution, we believe, is changing your recruitment processes: advertise all your roles as flexible and you will attract those returners – and more. And you can always provide some intensive coaching to those who may require it after a long career break.

Managers also need to be supported to really understand the nature of each job and what the expectations should be in terms of output. Historically, it may have been about someone working forty-five hours a week; turn that on its head and instead break the job down into tasks and activities, and understand how much of their time they will spend delivering these objectives. Critically, if you are going to have a conversation with someone about doing 80% of that role, which activities do you take out?

Also to be factored in is that we all function at different levels: some people may be able to perform more intensively than others. Therefore, it's about understanding what your expectations are in terms of outputs and performance from an individual within a role, and then adjusting that if you want to change the hours. If you get performance right and you understand the nature of job design, you can work out how to divide jobs up much more effectively.

Because we're currently in this request/response mode, where an individual has to ask to work less, there's a responsibility on both sides to think of the effect on the team: if you are taking five hours out of a job, where do those five hours go? Do they get dispersed among the rest of the team; in which case, are they happy with that? Do they not get done because, actually, you can afford to lose that activity? Do they get done as the person performs more efficiently, because they're working from home and not getting bothered by lots of phone calls? Or do you need to find somebody else in that team to pick up those five hours?

That's the reason why we have these conversations about 'floodgates'. Managers are rightly worried that you can get to a tipping point: you have five people in your team and everybody wants to work 0.8 – and there's a whole job that you've lost. But as long as you can face up to that, you can think about resourcing things differently.

Managers also need to work with finance to have the freedom and flexibility to do this: we need to start thinking more creatively about how to measure on full-time equivalent rather than headcount. If you have ten people in your team rather than seven because you've got three people job-sharing, that may be costing you a little bit more, but you'll be delivering far more output as a result.

Do we value part-time workers enough?

The evidence shows that the main driver for the gender pay gap is women choosing to work part time, and women are less likely to be promoted when they work part time. Behind that is an inherent assumption that, because they are working part time, they are less committed and therefore of less value, so it's a circle. But there are some deeper issues. Unless you redesign expectations for part-time workers, they often get measured on the same metrics as full-time workers, with the risk that they are recorded as being less productive and effective. That means that, as well as being seen as 'not committed 100% to my business', they are perceived as not performing as well.

The fact that, increasingly, men are asking to go part time for a better work/life balance or to share care responsibilities offers the hope that – eventually – this will be less of a gender issue. We know from research that many younger men would choose flexibility over remuneration in their next job.

This should wake business leaders up to the fact that this really is a talent issue: if you don't get this right, you should be worried that you will start to lose men from your business as well as women. However, even in this current crisis there is evidence that in dual-income households that are having to deal with home-schooling and balance life and work, working women currently spend an average of fifteen hours a week more on unpaid domestic labour than men.[96] What women need is for more men to be living and feeling that experience. And it's not just about caring for kids. Older people too have major caring responsibilities – and around one in three people in the workforce is aged fifty and over.[97]

The Covid-19 crisis has shone a very harsh light on our institutional framework that allows people to work and care. Take away schools, nurseries and various forms of social care, and you realise that we need all this infrastructure in order to work. We must recognise that in business we are only able to get people to work if they are able to fit work around everything else that's going on in their lives, and that we will get much more out of them if we can help them get that balance right.

Is progress being made?

The fact that, increasingly, businesses are coming to us to ask for advice and support shows progress. When we started fifteen years ago we didn't have a lot of the legislation that we have in place today. Flexibility has now landed.

We show a 'maturity curve' in our presentations to illustrate the journey of how businesses can go from being inherently 'reactive' – and giving permission to the odd person to work flexibly – through to being systemically 'flexible'. The companies coming to us for advice recognise that they are still near the start of the journey and that they need to work at it. And that's an important message. You don't just change behaviour and culture overnight. You don't just tell a manager to design a job differently and it happens, or expect a manager to suddenly manage a dispersed team of twenty-five people who they don't see from day to day. That requires vision, principles and a big shift from simply having a flexible working policy to actually having a strategy. Because this is about organisational design, and it's about behaviour.

Sometimes businesses don't act because they're worried about not being able to have a 'one size fits all' solution across all teams and disciplines, and that doesn't feel fair. But there's a big difference between equality and fairness, and if you can shift the culture to one that is proactive rather than reactive and encourage teams to talk about how they are working, you can start to flesh out and assuage some of those anxieties.

We run training sessions for middle managers and, when they are given the forum to think and talk about making it work, they often come up with the solutions themselves. It's about businesses giving managers permission to try different things, particularly at the point of hire.

Headhunters and recruitment agencies can play a role in changing company attitudes – and many are starting to do that – but it's fundamentally the responsibility of the business to be open to that conversation.

That is our big, big message. If you want to get great people into your business, why are you not having this conversation about flexibility with your candidates, in the same way as you would with people already in your organisation?

Five things to do

1. Do an audit of how your business has coped with home working during the pandemic: what were the challenges, failures, successes and drawbacks? Get feedback from *all* your staff on their experiences.

2. Ask all your staff what level of flexibility they would like to have in the future and what resources they would need to achieve that. Also ask your clients for feedback on their experience

of working with you during Covid-19, and their expectations of services provided by your client-facing staff in the future.

3. Explore the long-term cost benefits of introducing smart working. Include savings on space and other operational costs, as well as any potential extra spending that would be required to manage your business.

4. Consult HR and your recruitment agencies on how you can build flexibility into the specification of every new job you advertise. Tell your existing staff that job flexibility will be available after Covid-19, as long as it is feasible, and make it reason-neutral.

5. Develop a long-term strategy to make smart working the default practice in your business. In that process, include the line managers who will be implementing any changes.

SEVEN

The Diversity Project

'It's a sign of the times that over 1,000 people registered
to attend this year's Diversity Project annual event,
Time4inclusion – and encouraging that over 70% see
Covid-19 as more of an opportunity than a threat to
diversity and inclusion in the investment industry. It's
up to us to seize this moment: the industry needed a big
shake-up and we certainly have that now.'

— Baroness Helena Morrissey DBE, Financier[98]

Throughout this book, I have referenced the Diversity
Project as the organisation leading the way on cham-
pioning a more inclusive culture in the investment
and savings profession. Their story began in early
2016, when a group of leaders in the profession recognised that having an inclusive culture is important for
future success for their clients, members, employers
and shareholders, and decided to accelerate progress
towards this. That initiative led to the Diversity Project,
which has since made huge strides in raising awareness
of the issues and galvanising support for their aims.

Initially, the Diversity Project coordinated research involving twenty-four asset-management firms and nearly 4,000 individuals. The results confirmed what they already knew: the dominance of men in asset management and portfolio management; the high proportion of privately educated people in the industry; the low number of Black employees; and the low number of people who would describe themselves as disabled – relative to the working population as a whole.

Today, the Diversity Project has eighty member firms, including asset owners, investment managers, consulting firms and wealth managers. It also has thirty partners and supporters, which include industry bodies, search firms, diversity and inclusion consultancies and social enterprises. Together, they have built a large annual programme of events supported by reports, guides and videos to help member firms on their journey.

This chapter looks in more detail at the thinking that inspired its creation, the people behind it and where it plans to go from here.

The founders

The Diversity Project was forged by a small group of people who were determined to use their experiences to make sure that progressing a career would be easier for the next generation than it had been for them. Its roots were in gender diversity, but it soon became something far wider reaching. I asked Jane Welsh, Sarah Bates, Alexandra Haggard and Helena Morrissey what inspired them to set up the Diversity Project. Here are their stories.

Sarah Bates, Non-Executive Director

What were your early experiences in the sector?

I went to state school – although it was a direct-grant grammar school – and then Cambridge. In 1980, when I graduated, there were very few jobs going, but it was just at the time when UK brokers were looking for research analysts. No one in my family had ever worked in anything to do with finance, but it sounded interesting, and off I went.

Interestingly, when I joined, there were no established career paths in the broking, savings and investment business; it was rather more eccentric than that, less stratified. You didn't have to have read the City pages of whatever newspaper from the age of twelve, had work experience in lots of grand firms, or joined the City Club at university. So, arguably, in some ways, it was more open to certain groups than it later became.

There were some pretty senior women fund managers around the place when I started at a UK insurance company – better than it is now. I went to a predecessor company of Invesco as a fund manager, then became head of UK equities, before a brief spell as chief operating officer. After I'd had our daughter in 1993, I ran the investment trusts and other specialist divisions and then became CEO of the institutional business in the UK.

In common with other women at that time, when I had my first child I only took three months' maternity leave – at that point, there was only statutory maternity pay (about £90 a week for six weeks) to fall back on, so choices were somewhat limited. But at the time, it didn't seem that odd.

Have you met with sexism along the way?

I remember my first boss telling me soon after I started, 'You'll have to be a bit less girly.' I've never been particularly 'girly'. I just think he was trying to express something…God knows what it was. I've run across that time after time, including at the board of a fairly major company, when the outgoing chairman said: 'We interviewed another one of you…' I didn't realise what he meant until about twenty-four or forty-eight hours later.

In my first few jobs, people would say to me: 'Oh, you have to be much better to get anywhere if you're a woman.' People also talk about tokenism. I've been appointed to chair eleven different organisations – from charities and not-for-profits to investment trust boards and a FTSE 100 company – and seven of those were from having been a board member.

So, I have to assume that was on merit rather than tokenism.

Why did you start the Diversity Project?

I was sitting at some fund manager's entertainment do, and this chap from a big firm told me that only 13% of their graduate applicants were female. I asked why, and he said it was because they recruit largely mathematicians and then put them through a bear-pit recruitment process. And I thought, well, that's not really a starter, is it? A, it's pretty culturally biased; B, there *are* women mathematicians; and C, if you're putting people off with your recruitment processes, isn't there something wrong with them?

So, I checked that stat out with a couple of fund managers at big fund-management firms and they too came up with 13–14%. Some firms do better, but that's still worse than when I started.

I really hate the intern systems where friends of Mummy and Daddy get you jobs – that's really dysfunctional. We are trying to be objective, trying to be fair, but we've ended up with processes that defeat part of their objective. We have a belief that we are picking the best people, with a rather dodgy definition of what 'best' actually means.

All these people who say, 'We want the best person for the job' are not thinking things through. What you really want is the person who is going to make the group do better.

I remember asking a senior colleague about who had contributed most on his board during the crash, and he said it was the people who had, hitherto, been the most 'difficult'. They were the ones who responded most rapidly and most objectively to changing facts, not the people who had been the most collegiate.

After that, I spent some time trying to recruit people who were more disruptive to the boards I was involved with, and I have learned that it's important that disruptors understand how to influence as well: there's a fine line between being disruptive and being destructive.

I got Jane and Alexandra together for lunch, and we had a collective rant. Alexandra got the bit between her teeth and rang up Helena, who came up with this structure which doesn't have a 'command and control': as we would be relying on volunteers, it wasn't going to happen otherwise.

We set up the workstreams and some took off immediately because of the combined passion of a small group of people; some didn't, or took more time. But overall, it has worked because of its flexible structure – and that was Helena's great gift.

How do you see the pandemic changing the trajectory of the Diversity Project?

Some of what is going on will make a profound difference to enabling greater diversity and inclusion in the workplace – working from home, for instance, which is different from what people have been telling us over the last fifteen or twenty years. That should make a huge difference to people who are disabled, and those with more complicated lives for whatever reason.

However, I do think there's a danger that in times of crisis people tend to hunker down and go back to their own tribes. People will say, 'We can't be doing things that are seen as luxuries,' and some bits of diversity can be seen like that. Another thing that's happened in this crisis is that the benefits of different sorts of resilience are becoming quite obvious, and having to cope with the current situation may make people more aware of the benefits of cognitive diversity.

What would success in ten years' time look like for the Diversity Project?

We wouldn't have to exist.

Jane Welsh, Management Consultant

How did you get into the sector?

I started straight out of university, marketing early versions of portfolio risk analysis to asset managers and owners. Looking back, I was something of an oddity: a young woman in a world that was predominantly male and a lot older than me. And they definitely had different accents to mine!

When I moved to a US consulting company, I set up their first manager research capability in the UK and began an MBA at around the same time. I was always interested in group dynamics and what makes a good team. I was quite taken with the concept of groupthink and observing teams that seemed to spar off each other: people who brought different things to the table versus teams that looked like clones. I was looking for evidence of internal challenge within investment teams.

My work with trustee boards also helped me understand how it feels to be the outsider. And, again, when I went to a global consulting company, I moved into the world of actuaries, where I was definitely the outsider within a monoculture: mostly men; all mathematicians; all very smart. Around 2011 or 2012, my interest in diversity led to me chairing the company's inclusion and diversity council, which was looking at how we attracted, retained, developed and promoted diverse talents, specifically how we gave opportunities to some people but not to others.

At 'the lunch' with Sarah and Alexandra that started it all off, we asked ourselves: if we started out today, would we even get a job in the industry? Not only because of the way that big firms recruit at graduate level, focusing on particular universities and people with particular subject backgrounds, but also self-selection by students. If only a narrow range of people was bothering to apply, this raised concerns about the potential narrowing of cognitive diversity.

Right from the initial conversation, we were looking to include other groups as well as gender. Ethnicity and LGBT were included very early on, and every now and then a new area gets added because people are passionate about that dimension, and there are enough people to pursue it. We're a very 'bottom up' organisation, and it's worked by finding someone who is very passionate about a particular issue and helping them find friends who are similarly passionate and letting them get on with it.

Where does the project go from here?

A few years on, we still have a huge distance to go. What we're pushing for is culture change if we're to create more inclusive organisations, and that obviously has to come from the top. But we're also targeting some of our efforts at how we can support line managers, who are key to this. They're doing what they've been told to do – focusing on output – and they haven't always been supported to spend time creating an inclusive culture.

The end benefit to companies is cognitive diversity within the business. The evidence suggests that if you have a group of people who all think alike, even if they are smart, they are going to miss things. If you have a group of people who look at the world differently, and if people listen to those different viewpoints, which is always the challenge, there's a chance that they might pick up some of those risks or opportunities.

How can businesses begin to address this? Start with the data, because a lot of companies are in denial.

They may have gender data, but often very little else. And it's not just about staff numbers: you need to see what your retention rates are like for each category and how each progresses. Then it's a matter of making this part of the business strategy, seeing it as who they are as an organisation and what they want to be.

It can't just be a nice little thing that they add on at the end. It's got to come from the top, and a lot of leaders do get this – but they have got to live and breathe it, and make sure that the everyday experience aligns. Many companies say they do diversity and inclusion... but staff are still expected to make calls at four in the morning.

Alexandra Haggard, Head of Product and Investment Services

How did you begin your career?

I started out as an intern at a US consulting company in 2002. I was very fortunate to have a series of super managers, who helped me progress rapidly through the ranks. In August 2008, I was promoted to running the product development and product management team.

At that point, I had an awakening. I found myself regularly in the room with the executive committee, and they had a certain number of things in common. They were all male, at least ten years older than I was... and had wives who didn't work. They were all wonderful people – some have become lifelong friends – but I was very different from them.

The biggest impact of this difference was that I couldn't get my voice heard. I happened at the time to meet the most extraordinary woman: Anna Ostergren, an acting coach and theatre director. I learned to use my voice and body differently so that I would actually be seen and heard in these meetings. I'm lucky that what it took me was an investment in acting coaching; unfortunately, it would take something more revolutionary for others to be heard in our meeting rooms.

Why did you get involved in the Diversity Project?

In 2013 I was headhunted to be the CEO of a small US investment-consulting firm with incredible connections – including Helena. I've been very fortunate that Sarah Bates has been my mentor since 2008. She and I had been debating what to do about the diversity challenge. She introduced me to her great friend, Jane Welsh, and the three of us got together. When we later discussed it with Helena, it was clear that she had been thinking something quite similar, so we had an instant meeting of the minds.

The organisation has always been quite grassroots. If you've got a good idea, you use the project as an umbrella and get on with it. I've played a number of different roles – I'm leading the Disability workstream now and enjoying the opportunity we have to drive change in an area that still needs so much more work. I feel an enormous amount of pride for what has been achieved. We've helped to amplify the conversation, capitalise on some very difficult moments in society and find a way to make them more positive and turn them into change.

Where do we need to go from here?

We need more women, we need more Black people, we need more people in the industry who are disabled, and so many other cognitively diverse people. There's still masses to do, but I think we're now having much better conversations – and I think they are being had in different places.

We have to be really focused on making sure that it's actions, not words. But now is when we have the opportunity to make the most change, because it is unquestionably an inflection point in society.

Helena Morrissey, Chair

How did your involvement with the Diversity Project begin?

Setting up the 30% Club introduced the idea of pressing the case for more women at a senior level, but it was only at board level and it was only women. And while I had been involved in setting up a women's network inside my own firm, I hadn't felt able to go beyond that and look at diversity in the round.

It wasn't until 2016 when Alexandra Haggard, Jane Welsh and Sarah Bates came to see me and I felt that – yes, now was the time. They are all wonderful successes in their own parts of the industry, and all were genuinely concerned we were going backwards when it came to diversity and inclusion.

Before the 2007/2008 crisis, it was hard to make a case on business grounds for having more women. There was talk about equal opportunities, diversity and inclusion networks, and affinity groups, that sort of thing, but I always thought it made no sense to only have people from a very narrow educational background as well as the same gender, same geography, same social class, friends with each other: it's very difficult for them to challenge each other. It's not human nature. Part of their identity is the group they associate with, and we're not programmed to undermine our own group.

We're saying the fund-management industry isn't diverse in any dimension: socio-economic, ethnicity, disability, gender and so forth. It's diversity across the piece. Now we have a sense of urgency about it, and we're looking at every stage of the career, every aspect of the problem, I am confident that we will get some breakthroughs in underlying areas.

Sadly, there is no silver bullet, but I think one of the problems generally for the industry is that it's not well known – people don't know someone who works in it – so we have to go out more and be in schools and universities, team up with other people in the City and create a programme. Give them work experience before university.

Relative to any stage in our past, there is genuine desire for change at the very top – but diversity still wouldn't, for instance, be a regular item on the agenda in strategy meetings, or board discussions. For some chairs and CEOs, diversity is something for when you've got spare time and there are no other crises to deal with.

I've been hard at work on some of these issues for fifteen years. There's always a reason to prioritise something else – a currency crisis, Brexit, an election, Coronavirus – but if we'd never bothered, we'd still be stuck in the Dark Ages. We have to be careful about pushing it too hard in one sense, because there are a lot of hurdles to get over and we need sustained energy and commitment – it's easy for people to feel they've 'been there, done that' when there's still so much to do.

What would you see as success for the Diversity Project?

Being an industry that is vibrant, futureproof, looks and feels very different…and you wouldn't know it from another sector. Part of achieving those objectives will mean more people stepping up as mentors. Everyone who has made it to some sort of level in our industry has had some sort of ally or mentor along the way. No one is an island; and if you're not powerful, you ideally need someone who is more powerful to be your mentor.

We have to not just redouble our existing efforts but refine them. And we'll be refreshing the messages – not just banging people over the head. They have to see that it's what they want, not just what they're expected or pressured to do. But it is still only baby steps. We need a big 'whoosh', so you don't even think about diversity any more.

The Diversity Project's Manifesto for Change

In this section, the Diversity Project speaks for itself: this is their vision, together with the commitments they expect member companies to stand by to help them achieve that vision.

We believe that we have an extraordinary opportunity to press the reset button in our industry: to recruit, nurture and retain the first truly diverse generation of savings and investment professionals.

That generation will themselves perpetuate diversity in our industry; we are looking to break one cycle and create another. If we are successful, in the next four years:

- Our businesses will better reflect both society at large, and the individuals who trust us with their money

- Our people will create better financial outcomes to benefit our diverse savers and investors

- We will attract more interest in the industry, with a pipeline of diverse talent

Diversity is not only our social obligation, it's a business imperative.

Vision

A truly diverse and inclusive UK investment and savings industry with the right talent to deliver the best possible results for our clients and to reflect the society we serve.

Commitment to progress

To achieve this, we encourage all asset-management, wealth-management and investment-consulting firms to commit to achieving the following standards and to monitor progress towards the achievement of the standards. We ask firms to monitor and report on their progress towards fulfilling these standards on an annual basis on a 'comply or explain' basis using the self-assessment template which includes the criteria for achieving a green rating on each of the standards.

The completion of this self-assessment provides a useful framework for assessing your organisation's diversity and inclusion credentials. For example, some firms are using this as part of demonstrating to their board their compliance with the Senior Managers Regime. For others it will be helpful in identifying priority areas for action and for benchmarking progress.

In addition, we believe that collating the results across the industry can help inform what the priorities for the Diversity Project should be for the year ahead and to benchmark progress.

Standards

1. The senior leaders in our firm have included diversity in their personal objectives.

2. We measure and monitor the diversity of our employees (eg age, gender, ethnicity, sexual orientation, disability) and report this data regularly to the executive committee and board.

3. We have a diversity and inclusion strategy appropriate to the business which includes measurable objectives.

4. Both the strategy, and progress towards it, are reviewed annually by the management team, shared with employees and adjustments made to the programme as necessary.

5. As appropriate, we have reviewed practices around recruitment, promotions, mentoring and sponsorship opportunities, work allocation (eg how portfolios are allocated among fund managers or how project or client teams are put together), parental leave, pay generally and agile working – for all staff – to promote an inclusive culture.

6. We have published the gender pay gap, along with our plan to address the underlying causes where a gap exists. We have sought to identify any other pay gaps which might exist (eg ethnic pay gap).

7. We actively contribute to the Diversity Project (eg be involved in two or more Diversity Project workstreams and are represented at the Steering Committee or Advisory Council).

8. We have taken part in any relevant benchmarking surveys or research initiatives.

9. We have worked collaboratively with others to share experience and worked to help tackle common barriers to diversity.

10. We have provided constructive feedback to the Diversity Project where more focus or a new approach is needed.

The investment and savings industry perspective

The irony is not lost on those striving for change that businesses in the investment and savings industry regularly vet companies for their sustainability and ethical integrity on behalf of their clients, applying metrics on employee diversity that they aren't always achieving themselves.

I talked to Diversity Project ambassador Helen Price from Brunel Pension Partnership about the perspective of the pension funds, institutional investors, family offices and retail investors – the asset owners – and whether pressure from them could drive greater inclusivity.

Helen Price, Diversity Project Ambassador

Asset owners who are committed to diversity can wield significant influence to ensure the companies managing their assets are equally committed. For instance, at the pension fund where I lead on stewardship, engagement and voting, our approach is to routinely ask asset managers about diversity within their companies as part of ongoing monitoring.

However, it's difficult to ascertain what 'good' actually looks like. It's easy enough for a company to give us their policy, tell us they've got employee groups and assure us they think diversity is 'important'. It's a lot harder to assess whether diversity and inclusion are embedded appropriately or not, and whether the theme is being taken seriously.

Making comparisons between different companies, or setting up league tables, is, theoretically, one way forward, but that's also problematic because an international business will have different policies for each territory. There will be differences between various industry areas, and that's before you start to think about the size of the asset manager. For example, within a larger company, each member represents a small percentage of the population – and vice versa. Also, if you have one company with a lower starting point, they could consistently be at the bottom of the diversity rankings, even though they are making progress versus a company which had less to do. You can have varying levels of diversity at different levels within a company. Quantitative information can be really useful as a signal to have a conversation, but you also need the qualitative story for the whole picture.

All that said, in general terms, I'd say that the situation is improving across the asset-management industry. One of the great strengths of the Diversity Project is that we are able to speak candidly to individuals from a range of different companies who are passionate about inclusion and diversity, and find out from them the challenges they are facing and how they are tackling them.

Historically, there was not a lot of public information. You wouldn't see it on their website, and it was hard to tell from the outside what the industry baseline was. The Diversity Project gives you access to what some of those policies might be. The project also gives us access to information that we can feed back internally, enabling us to look at ourselves: how we are handling diversity and what improvements we can make. It's about sharing best practice or sharing challenges and solutions.

For example, one discussion being held within the asset managers' group is around the change on how you certify people within the industry. Now we have moved to the senior management certification regime, there are questions over, for example, whether someone who's away for twelve weeks is still classified as a certified person.

Asset managers are interpreting that in different ways – especially around maternity, enhanced paternity or shared parental leave. Some say that if you've been away you need to be recertified; others say that, since you've always been here, you don't need anything new. As a result of this issue being flagged up, individuals within the group went back to their compliance teams and were able to share the approaches they were taking. Moreover, the group raised this with the FCA as a potential issue. It certainly is not the intention of the FCA to create any barriers to diversity.

How do you separate out those that are polishing their policies for your benefit from those actually making cultural change?

Within our firm, there will be initial questions within the tender exercise, and you can see quite quickly whether they have policies in place. With those that don't, it's normally a signal that it's not something that they are looking at. Then, when we take the asset manager through to the next stages, we do due diligence and question them a lot more on the detail. For instance: whether they have information around key performance indicators; whether they have tied it into remuneration of employees; and who's got ownership – the board and partners, or those lower down, such as middle managers?

That level of information can give you an indication of how seriously they are taking it.

How committed, for instance, are they to things like the Women in Finance Charter[99] and the more recent Race at Work Charter?[100] These are good, constructive initiatives because, if you sign up to a charter, you have to set targets and annually disclose your performance against them. Some of the more progressive asset managers (I'm not saying all of them!) tend to be signed up to these initiatives as well as to initiatives such as the Diversity Project and the 30% Club.[101]

But there are other questions worth asking, too. For instance, are they working with organisations like

Investment 20/20,[102] or targeting specific groups
for internships? What are they doing to improve the
perception of the industry? How many of their staff
have actually taken up enhanced leave? How many
have returned? Do they know how long their staff
stay for after they've been on leave? Is there enough
support in place for returning staff?

Digging deeper at the due diligence stage means you
soon get to the bottom of whether policies are being
followed through.

*Are you pushing at an open door or meeting resistance
around diversity?*

The door is certainly more open than it was before:
specifically, it's easier to have conversations around
gender diversity. However, you still sometimes
hear: 'We've put one female on the board, now stop
talking about it.' Or: 'We've done these assessments
and we've got great diversity of thought: so-and-so
(who happens to be a white male) spent two weeks in
South-East Asia.'

But diversity is a continually evolving theme. Over
the last year, I've seen more asset managers realise
that this could actually be a very useful thing for them.
We've seen the launch of investments specifically
targeted at diversity, indices that target diversity, and
impact funds as well, including some that support
women in less developed countries. However, we
do still get pushback – most often from the US – and
here it comes down to a legal and data-sharing

perspective. There is concern around data privacy,
yes, but also over where we are going to compare
them with other asset managers. There are ways in
which data can be shared in line with the law, safely
and in pursuit of a common goal.

We are seeing improvements. Institutional
Shareholder Services (ISS)[103] wrote to the large UK
and US public companies over the summer of 2020
asking for greater disclosure around ethnicity data
and other diversity metrics,[104] and they've seen
some improvements. That information is now being
fed back. ISS, though, is a paid-for resource, and I do
question whether diversity data should be a paid-for
resource, as it could slow progress.

*What would progress over the next couple of years look
like to you?*

Greater disclosure from asset managers, and for
them to be taking a lead in providing that. Also, having
more asset owners as part of the Diversity Project.
I'm actually working with a group of asset owners
at the moment, and the idea is for a working group
to develop a pledge or charter, with the objective
to formalise a set of actions that asset owners can
commit to in order to improve diversity, in all its
forms, across the investment industry, and lead to a
more consistent and common approach.

Often there is pressure to consolidate diversity and
inclusion questions during the tender process, so the
group is developing a questionnaire which will enable

a range of questions to be asked during ongoing manager monitoring.

We're also working with other groups in this field with the hope that, within a year, we can pull all of this data together and create a report, assessing where we are. That would enable asset owners to look at individual managers and determine whether or not they even want to consider them as part of a tender assessment.

If we can do this, it would send a clear, strong message that asset owners take diversity seriously.

EIGHT

Build Back Better

'This pandemic has forced a change in momentum upon us; now is the opportunity to accelerate positive change. With such an uncertain outlook, it is more important than ever to embrace inclusivity and diversity to enable business resilience and to build back better.'

— Jayne Styles,
   Ambassador Workstream Leader[105]

This book was written during the throes of a pandemic, when major logistical changes had to be effected swiftly and securely to enable the investment and savings sector to continue functioning. That proved to be a success. What became clear in the months that followed were the long-term ramifications of Covid-19 for diversity and inclusion, not least because successfully finding 'new ways of doing things' has pushed aside arguments that have long acted as barriers to change. Once 'normality' returns, we could revert to the old way of doing things, but I don't think that's going to happen. The genie is well and truly out of the bottle.

In July 2020, the Diversity Project published a report entitled *The Build Back Better Diversity Project* written by Jayne Styles,[106] who leads the Ambassador workstream. This report recognises that positives can, and should, be drawn from what has been a tumultuous and damaging year in so many ways. As the preface makes clear:

> 'Whilst the outlook remains unclear and businesses face many challenges, there are also real opportunities to reshape the future and for the investment industry to emerge stronger, more resilient, and modernised.

> 'Rapid change has already happened, and people are expecting more, so let us seize this moment. Inclusivity and diversity are enablers to building back better. With a strong sense that feelings of corporate inclusion have risen during the crisis, we need to leverage this momentum, as there is still a long way to go.'

A life-threatening pandemic has forced society to work in different ways and re-evaluate many of its priorities. Many businesses are also facing severe financial pressures: not always the ideal setting for advancing cultural shifts which are seen as long-term investments. Already in some parts of the economy we are seeing echoes of the financial crash of 2008, where businesses adopted extensive cost-saving activities in an effort to survive. In the main, this led to draconian HR practices such as compulsory redundancies, simplifying contracts, outsourcing and deskilling.

What, then, might an investment and savings sector built back in a *better* way look like, and what are the keys to achieving that? Importantly, how should business leaders shape their strategies as restrictions ease while ensuring the fight for equality is not lost?

My approach is to look at it through the lens of 'ambidextrous leadership' – loosely defined as simultaneously harnessing explorative and exploitative approaches. In this context, 'exploration' embraces experimentation and innovation, while 'exploitation' focuses on refinement and implementation.

Ambidextrous leadership

Put simply, two polar opposites are at play in ambidextrous leadership: exploration and exploitation.

- Explorative practices are linked with transformational leadership: innovation, experimentation, flexibility and expanding into 'the unknown' (eg new products and markets).

- Exploitative approaches focus on aspects of transactional leadership: efficiency, reducing costs and keeping within 'the known' (eg reducing creative practices and risk).

In times of crisis, many organisations are drawn towards exploitative practices to survive, but ignoring the potential of an explorative approach would be to jettison what we have learned from the pandemic. It has given us the opportunity to get off the conveyor belt and question old practices: particularly important because so many people are keen not to return to the old normal, but to create a positive 'new' one.

Ambidextrous leadership isn't about choosing one approach over another, but combining the two. This can be done in a way that will strengthen our sector for the long term while enhancing our ability to survive in the short term. This creates a paradoxical and theoretical set of tensions; but, as the *Build Back Better* report highlights, embracing flexible leadership approaches is essential for making progress towards equality in the workplace. It can play a key role in:

- Attracting and retaining talent
- Fostering strong company loyalty
- Improving employee wellbeing
- Improving operational efficiency

Moreover, this need not be incompatible with the drive to make savings and reduce overheads.

How to build back better

In light of the challenges faced by the sector, the report looks through the lens of diversity and inclusion to focus on four key areas: working location, wellbeing, culture and flexibility.

Working location

Many people have welcomed working from home and have largely come to terms with the 'new normal' of flexible working – including video calling and conferencing – and the financial sector has rapidly adapted. It has enabled many to combine care duties, achieve a better work/life balance or reduce the hours they commute. However, it has not been welcomed by employees whose circumstances are not well suited to remote working, and some have found the situation stressful and isolating.

The report highlights that by building more remote working into a company's HR strategy, costs could be saved by reducing workspace allocations for employees and closing or shrinking expensive national offices in favour of regional hubs. Careful planning is needed for the post-lockdown return to work, though. If you want to take a new blended approach to working locations, it's critical to consider the implications for *all* groups of employees and how they support this changing environment. For example, encourage employees to agree a daily schedule with their partners that allows childcare shifts to be arranged around work, and to agree with their manager times of the day when they won't be available. Similarly, older workers with caring responsibilities may need a flexible approach to their work patterns and management. Managers should focus on productivity, rather than number of hours worked.

In an article for the *Harvard Business Review*, Roberts and McCluney highlight that working from home presents an additional challenge for Black employees, who regularly manage their professional image by code-switching: using one language (or variety of language) at work and another with family.[107] The video-calling technology widely used during lockdown removes Black employees' choice about how they present themselves. To address this issue, encourage the social norm of video backgrounds and give people the option to have their cameras off during larger meetings.

Wellbeing

During the crisis, well-established office environments and routines were replaced by the isolation of home. For some, this sudden change has increased anxiety and stress around aspects such as safety, control and human connection. This has led many employers to actively publicise their employee assistance schemes, make mental health first aiders available and schedule company-wide self-care days.

These are measures that need to continue after Covid-19 – and when planning their wellbeing strategy, employers should consider specific support for younger workers and women. Social relationships at work are a major source of job satisfaction and support; losing these has been a significant negative for many employees. These issues can be exaggerated for younger employees, as Kłopotek[108] found when researching the experience of younger employees working from home. According to Kłopotek's research, the key issues for this group are difficulty in separating home affairs from professional ones, and social isolation. To support this group, employers need to establish and nurture virtual social networks, buddy schemes and virtual 'let's talk' sessions to encourage colleagues to share tips for dealing with issues.

Women have been disproportionally impacted by the stresses of juggling multiple competing demands during lockdown. Research during the lockdown period by King's College London[109] highlights that female parents are spending seven hours in an average weekday on childcare, compared with five hours for male parents. This may explain why during lockdown 53% of women have felt more anxious and depressed than usual.[110] To take account of this imbalance, employers need to consider providing informal time off, encouraging all employees to take short breaks, such as an afternoon every week or a full day here and there, for family time. Managers need to respect this time off.

Culture

The Diversity Project's paper identifies that during the lockdown period, empathy in companies has increased and corporate cultures have become more inclusive. As a result, employees' expectations have risen – meaning that a return to the way things used to be done would reduce morale and loyalty and make it harder for companies to retain staff.

This is directly connected to the diversity and inclusion agenda. In this competitive environment, the report argues that companies should do the following:

1. Commit to diversity and inclusion by aligning values and executive support and by signing up for charters that require action.

2. Role-model through executive behaviour, storytelling, normalising flexible working and committing to inclusive leadership by being compassionate, kind and curious about staff.

3. Implement visible, well-funded diversity and inclusion strategies with measurable key performance indicators on collective and individual performance.

Flexibility

In its final chapter, the Diversity Project's report identifies that the Covid-19 crisis has helped break down historic resistance from line managers by proving that companies can operate remotely. It's now important to emphasise the positives and reinforce that the option of remote working is now the norm. To make the workplace truly flexible, though, there is still a need to take simple 'working from home' further. The Diversity Project's *Manifesto for Change*[111] proposes five key actions to achieve this:

1. CEOs must be seen to champion flexible working, to set the vision and cultural tone of the organisation.

2. Flexible working arrangements will be reason-neutral.

3. Flexibility will be designed into jobs as standard.

4. Managers will be supported to build their capabilities to manage flexible and dispersed teams.

5. Managers should take a proactive approach to reviewing flexible working arrangements.'

Keeping the focus on diversity and inclusion the *Build Back Better* report gives us a lot to think about in terms of leadership practice and continuing to work towards equality through and beyond Covid-19.

The recommendations in the report might not be easy to put in place, but an ambidextrous leadership approach will help. Leaders should not be thinking in terms of 'either/or': the emphasis is on finding excellence in both exploitative and explorative approaches.

Being resilient is crucial, as the report suggests, but it is also vital not to lose sight of the existing important organisational issues around equality in our attempts to adjust to – and survive – the changes resulting from Covid-19.

Conclusion

There has been growing recognition in society over the last few years of groups who struggle to feel fully included or accepted in the workplace.

As part of that shift, the scope of the Diversity Project has expanded significantly, with members stepping up to establish a whole series of workstreams. Progress is being made, but changes in culture and working practices are still needed. The personal stories of some of the workstream leaders not only shed light on the challenges and solutions, but also argue the case for more diversity in the investment and savings industry.

One of the most common concerns voiced by business leaders is how to recruit and retain people from these different groups – especially in smaller companies. One of the key messages of this book is that you can remove one common barrier by adopting more flexible working practices. The other simple starting point is to proactively celebrate diversity, and let your employees (and prospective ones) know that you are a business that values and welcomes *all* talented people.

Make that known on your website and to your recruitment agencies. Encourage and enable staff to create networks or to join those set up by the Diversity Project. Invite people from inside (or outside) your company to share their stories. This way, no one group feels left behind. It also opens the door to people in the business who think their group needs support, making it possible for them to come forward and have that important conversation.

For instance, in my own business I've become an ally for LGBT Great. We supported Pride Month with various activities, most significantly encouraging open conversations. The awards I mentioned at the beginning of the book are our way of saying to the marketplace: 'We care about this.' The people in our business can feel proud that we do.

The founders and the workstream leaders of the Diversity Project all recognise that, while progress has been made, more needs to be done to raise awareness of the urgent need for more diversity and inclusion in the investment and savings industry. This book is one part of a concerted, ongoing effort to 'move the dial', and the impact of Covid-19 will certainly accelerate progress. Ultimately, though, it will come down to business leaders and senior managers going beyond pledges and promises, and walking the walk.

Getting to the same stage that we have now reached with environmental, social and governance (ESG) may take a few years yet, but we will get there. Some business managers will reach that point because they recognise the fairness and equity that diversity and inclusion bring. Others will be pressed into action by clients expecting them to step up to the mark or risk losing their business. Yet more will look at the problems they're having with recruiting young talent and connect the dots.

Getting the messaging right is critical, because a wide range of people with different responsibilities and perspectives and motivations need to be won over. Linda Russheim, Marketing Consultant, has driven the Diversity Project's marketing strategy, and she explains:

'If we're talking to the CEOs of our members, the mention of P&Ls [profit and loss statements] definitely gets their attention.

'For others, the focus is more about culture and the concept of belonging, or just the right thing to do. If you look at the Diversity Project's manifesto, its primary focus is that we should get more diverse talent into the industry to ensure that we are doing the best for our clients, and that we are staying relevant, resilient and don't get disrupted.

'The importance of cognitive diversity is the message that ties all the work across the

Diversity Project together and has the benefit of resonating with the widest population. When we focus on the importance of having great talent and different perspectives, we get great engagement.

'Underneath cognitive diversity, the benefit is that each key group of stakeholders – asset owners, asset managers or consultants – can all find something that works for them, and that also works across the different aspects of diversity.'[112]

Linda's conclusion is also mine:

'To make long-term sustainable changes, with more companies treating diversity as a business imperative, we need to see cultural changes within organisations that nurture truly inclusive workplaces, to help get better results for customers, provide greater opportunities for diverse talent and create more resilient, successful organisations.'

Appendix:
The Diversity Project Charity

100% of the author's proceeds from this book will be donated to the Diversity Project Charity.[113]

The Diversity Project Charity is a grant-giving organisation. Their initial aim was to raise £2 million to help the charities who had been affected by the disbandment of the President's Club, as well as some regional charities focusing on inclusivity. Since 2020, they have been supporting charities with social mobility, diversity and inclusivity aims. The charity's grant-giving is guided by values and principles that underpin their work.

Diversity and inclusion: They believe in empowering people by respecting and appreciating what makes them different, in terms of age, gender, ethnicity, religion, disability, sexual orientation, education, thought and national origin.

Transparency: They ensure they work in an open and honest manner, providing full information required for collaboration and cooperation.

Respect: They seek to act with integrity, and to value privacy and confidentiality.

Collaboration: They believe in the value of working together and sharing ideas to produce the best results.

Purpose: They want to support and advance charitable causes in the UK and make a positive sustainable impact.

www.diversityprojectcharity.org

The Author

Steve Butler is a Chartered Manager and Companion of the Chartered Management Institute. He gained his master's in business administration from Solent University and is currently researching for his doctorate in business administration at the University of Winchester.

In his current role as business leadership and manager, academic researcher and industry diversity campaigner, he is a regular writer and speaker on intergenerational working, retirement and older worker business management issues. *Inclusive Culture: Leading change in organisations and industries* is Steve's third management book covering diversity and inclusion issues. His other books include *Manage The Gap: Achieving success with intergenerational teams* and *The Midlife Review: A guide to work, wealth and wellbeing.*

In 2019, Steve became a member of the Diversity Project Advisory Council and executive sponsor of the Smart Working workstream, and he is an active supporter of the project. He is chief executive of Punter Southall Aspire, a national retirement savings business with 150 employees.

🌐 www.psaspire.com
🔗 www.linkedin.com/in/stevenbutler

Notes

1 Diversity Project, 'About' (no date), https://diversityproject.com
/about, accessed 18 May 2021

2 ONS, *Ethnicity and National Identity in England and Wales* (Office for
National Statistics, 2012)

3 Diversity Project, '#TalkAboutBlack Workstream' (no date), https://
diversityproject.com/talkaboutblack, accessed 18 May 2021

4 Diversity Project, 'Diversity Project Sets New Ambitious Targets
for Women in Asset Management as Part of Commitments to
Build Back Better' (30 July 2020), https://diversityproject.com/2020
-07-30/diversity-project-sets-new-ambitious-targets-women-asset
-management-part-commitments

5 ONS, *Labour Force Survey Performance and Quality Monitoring
Report: January to March 2019* (Office for National Statistics, 2019),
www.ons.gov.uk/employmentandlabourmarket/peopleinwork
/employmentandemployeetypes/methodologies/labourforcesurve
yperformanceandqualitymonitoringreports/labourforcesurveyperf
ormanceandqualitymonitoringreportjanuarytomarch2019, accessed
18 May 2021

6 S Butler, *Manage The Gap: Achieving success with intergenerational
teams* (Rethink Press, 2019)

7 PJ Zak, 'Why Your Brain Loves Good Storytelling', *Harvard Business
Review* (28 October 2014), https://hbr.org/2014/10/why-your-brain
-loves-good-storytelling, accessed 15 March 2021

8 CIPD, 'Organisational Culture and Cultural Change' (CIPD, 2020)
www.cipd.co.uk/knowledge/culture/working-environment
/organisation-culture-change-factsheet, accessed 16 March 2021

9 CIPD, 'Inclusion and Diversity in the Workplace' (CIPD, 2021), www
.cipd.co.uk/knowledge/fundamentals/relations/diversity/factsheet,
accessed 7 June 2021

10 L Sherbin and R Rashid, 'Diversity Doesn't Stick Without Inclusion', *Harvard Business Review* (1 February 2017), https://hbr.org/2017/02/diversity-doesnt-stick-without-inclusion, accessed 18 May 2021

11 Equality and Human Rights Commission, 'Understanding Equality' (updated 2 August 2018), www.equalityhumanrights.com/en/secondary-education-resources/useful-information/understanding-equality, accessed 18 May 2021

12 I Gottesman, *Critical Race Theory and Legal Studies: The critical turn in education from Marxist critique to Poststructuralist Feminism to critical theories of race* (Taylor & Francis, 2016)

13 CIPD, 'Organisational Culture and Cultural Change'

14 CIPD, 'Organisational Culture and Cultural Change'

15 S Butler, *Manage The Gap*

16 S Butler, *Manage The Gap*

17 CIPD, 'Inclusion and Diversity in the Workplace' (updated 10 May 2021), www.cipd.co.uk/knowledge/fundamentals/relations/diversity/factsheet#6424, accessed 18 May 2021

18 Private interview, 4 August 2020

19 Diversity Project, 'Diversity Project Sets New Ambitious Targets for Women in Asset Management as Part of Commitments to Build Back Better'

20 BBC, 'Firms With More Female Executives Perform Better' (27 July 2020), www.bbc.co.uk/news/business-53548704, accessed 18 May 2021

21 J Clempner, M Daisley and A Jaekel, 'Women in Financial Services 2020' (Oliver Wyman, 2020), www.diversityproject.com/sites/default/files/resources/Women-In-Financial-Services-2020%20-%20report.pdf, accessed 18 May 2021

22 Diversity Project, 'Diversity Project Sets New Ambitious Targets for Women in Asset Management as Part of Commitments to Build Back Better'

23 Diversity Project, 'Diversity Project Sets New Ambitious Targets for Women in Asset Management as Part of Commitments to Build Back Better'

24 Diversity Project, 'Diversity Project Sets New Ambitious Targets for Women in Asset Management as Part of Commitments to Build Back Better'

25 City Hive, www.cityhive.co.uk, accessed 18 May 2021

26 Moving Ahead, https://moving-ahead.org, accessed 18 May 2021

27 Women Returners, https://womenreturners.com, accessed 18 May 2021

28 upReach, https://upreach.org.uk, accessed 18 May 2021

29 Timewise, https://timewise.co.uk, accessed 18 May 2021

30 Diversity Project, 'Gender Equality: Guidance for organisations' (no date), https://diversityproject.com/resource/gender-equality-guidance-organisations, accessed 18 May 2021

31 CIPD, 'Diversity and Inclusion at Work: Facing up to the business case' (CIPD, 2018), www.cipd.co.uk/knowledge/fundamentals /relations/diversity/diversity-inclusion-report, accessed 18 May 2021

32 Diversity Project, '#TalkAboutBlack Workstream' (2020), www .diversityproject.com/talkaboutblack, accessed 18 May 2021

33 ONS, *Ethnicity and National Identity in England and Wales*

34 Diversity Project, '#TalkAboutBlack Workstream'

35 Diversity Project, '#TalkAboutBlack Workstream'

36 L Noonan and TN Rogers, 'Share of Black Employees in Senior US Finance Roles Falls Despite Diversity Efforts', *Financial Times* (31 March 2021), www.ft.com/content/887d064a-bd5e-4ce6-9671 -9057e12bd5c7, accessed 18 May 2021

37 E Eddo-Lodge, *Why I'm No Longer Talking to White People About Race* (Bloomsbury, 2018)

38 Business in the Community, 'Race' (no date), www.bitc.org.uk/race, accessed 18 May 2021

39 CIPD, 'Barriers to BAME Employee Career Progression to the Top' (updated 4 December 2017), www.cipd.co.uk/knowledge /fundamentals/relations/diversity/bame-career-progression, accessed 18 May 2021

40 Panel discussion, 19 November 2020

41 B Chapman, 'UK Skills Shortage Could Cost £90bn Per Year With Brexit to Make Things Worse, Say Councils', *Independent* (5 July 2017), www.independent.co.uk/news/business/news/uk-skills -shortage-cost-90-billion-brexit-latest-news-lga-local-government -association-a7825061.html, accessed 18 May 2021

42 CIPD, 'Managing an Age-diverse Workforce: Employer and employee views' (CIPD, 2014), www.cipd.co.uk/Images/managing -an-age-diverse-workforce_2014_tcm18-10838.PDF, accessed 18 May 2021

43 S Butler and T Watts, *The Midlife Review: A guide to work, wealth and wellbeing* (Rethink Press, 2020)

44 NHS, 'Overview: Menopause' (updated 29 August 2018), www.nhs .uk/conditions/menopause, accessed 18 May 2021

45 CIPD, 'A Guide to Managing Menopause at Work: Guidance for line managers' (CIPD, 2021), www.cipd.co.uk/Images/menopause- guide-for-people-managers_tcm18-55548.pdf, accessed 18 May 2021

46 CIPD, 'A Guide to Managing Menopause at Work'

47 upReach, https://upreach.org.uk

48 CIPD, 'Age-diverse Workforces' (no date), www.cipd.co.uk/news -views/viewpoint/age-diversity, accessed 18 May 2021

49 Private interview, 17 August 2020

50 UK Government, 'Definition of Disability Under the Equality Act 2010' (no date), www.gov.uk/definition-of-disability-under-equality -act-2010, accessed 18 May 2021

51 A Powell, 'Disabled People in Employment: House of Commons Library Briefing Paper No 7540' (UK Parliament, April 2021), https://commonslibrary.parliament.uk/research-briefings/cbp-7540

52 Department for Work and Pensions, 'Guidance: Employing disabled people and people with health conditions' (updated 25 March 2020), www.gov.uk/government/publications/employing-disabled-people-and-people-with-health-conditions/employing-disabled-people-and-people-with-health-conditions, accessed 18 May 2021

53 N Walker, 'Neurodiversity: Some basic terms and definitions', Neurocosmopolitan blog (27 September 2014), https://neurocosmopolitanism.com/neurodiversity-some-basic-terms-definitions, accessed 18 May 2021

54 H Blume, 'Neurodiversity: On the neurological underpinnings of geekdom', *The Atlantic* (September 1998), www.theatlantic.com/magazine/archive/1998/09/neurodiversity/305909, accessed 18 May 2021

55 T Armstrong, *The Power of Neurodiversity: Unleashing the advantages of your differently wired brain* (DaCapo Lifelong/Perseus Books, 2011)

56 V Nimmo-Smith et al, 'Anxiety Disorders in Adults With Autism Spectrum Disorder: A population-based study', *Journal of Autism and Developmental Disorders*, 50/1 (2020), 308–318

57 Scope, www.scope.org.uk, accessed 16 March 2021

58 CIPD and Uptimize, 'Neurodiversity at Work' (CIPD, 2018), www.cipd.co.uk/Images/neurodiversity-at-work_2018_tcm18-37852.pdf, accessed 18 May 2021

59 CIPD and Uptimize, 'Neurodiversity at Work'

60 CIPD and Uptimize, 'Neurodiversity at Work'

61 CIPD, 'Disability and Employment' (updated February 2021), www.cipd.co.uk/knowledge/fundamentals/emp-law/disability-discrimination/factsheet, accessed 18 May 2021

62 Diversity Project, 'Neurodiversity: Top 10 tips' (Diversity Project, 2019), https://diversityproject.com/resource/neurodiversity-top-10-tips, accessed 18 May 2021

63 Autism Speaks, www.autismspeaks.org, accessed 16 March 2021

64 Spectrum Employment Community, by AASCEND (LinkedIn), www.linkedin.com/groups/5086843, accessed 18 May 2021

65 Private interview, 24 July 2020

66 Stonewall, 'Glossary of Terms' (no date), www.stonewall.org.uk/help-advice/faqs-and-glossary/glossary-terms, accessed 18 May 2021

67 ONS, 'Sexual Orientation, UK: 2017' (ONS, 2017), www.ons.gov.uk/peoplepopulationandcommunity/culturalidentity/sexuality/bulletins/sexualidentityuk/2017, accessed 18 May 2021

68 B Sears and C Mallory, 'Documented Evidence of Employment Discrimination & Its Effects on LGBT People' (The Williams Institute, University of California School of Law, 2011), https://

williamsinstitute.law.ucla.edu/publications/employ-discrim-effect
-lgbt-people, accessed 18 May 2021

69 JM Grant et al, 'Injustice at Every Turn: A report of the National
    Transgender Discrimination Survey', National Center for
    Transgender Equality and National Gay and Lesbian Task Force
    (2011), www.transequality.org/sites/default/files/docs/resources
    /NTDS_Report.pdf, accessed 18 May 2021

70 LGBT Great, 'Project 1000 Role Models' (no date), www.lgbtgreat
    .com/role-models, accessed 18 May 2021

71 LGBT Great, www.lgbtgreat.com, accessed 16 March 2021

72 InterInvest, https://interinvest.org, accessed 16 March 2021

73 The Investment Association, www.theia.org, accessed 16 March
    2021

74 LGBT Great, 'Project 1000 Role Models'

75 CIPD, 'Sexual Orientation, Gender Identity, Gender Reassignment
    and Employment' (CIPD, 2021), www.cipd.co.uk/knowledge
    /fundamentals/emp-law/sexual-orientation-discrimination
    /factsheet, accessed 18 May 2021

76 Private interview, 5 June 2020

77 Private interview, 4 August 2020

78 D Thomas, 'How the Pandemic Will Change the City Office',
    Financial Times (3 January 2021), www.ft.com/content/a399c208-7027
    -4138-abbf-6c08ef818a44, accessed 15 March 2021

79 Timewise, 'Flexible Working: A talent imperative' (Timewise,
    2017), https://timewise.co.uk/wp-content/uploads/2019/06
    /Flexible_working_Talent_Imperative.pdf, accessed 18 May 2021

80 Timewise, 'Timewise Flexible Jobs Index 2020' (Timewise, 2020),
    https://timewise.co.uk/article/flexible-jobs-index, accessed 18 May
    2021

81 Diversity Project, 'Addressing Barriers to Diversity in Portfolio
    Management: Performance and continuity management'
    (Diversity Project, 2019), https://diversityproject.com/sites/default
    /files/resources/Addressing-barriers-to-diversity-in-portfolio
    -management.pdf, accessed 15 March 2021

82 Financial Services Skills Taskforce, 'Financial Services Skills
    Taskforce: Final report' (TheCityUK, 2020), www.thecityuk.com
    /assets/2020/Reports/43e976fdcd/Financial-Services-Skills
    -Taskforce-final-report.pdf, accessed 15 March 2021

83 Aviva, 'Working Lives Report 2017' (Aviva 2017), www.aviva.co.uk
    /adviser/documents/view/workinglivesreport2017.pdf, accessed 15
    March 2021

84 Aviva, 'Working Lives Report 2017'

85 HSBC, 'People and Productivity: Flexible working' (2017), www
    .business.hsbc.uk/-/media/library/business-uk/pdfs/productivity
    -report-2017.pdf, accessed 18 May 2021

86 Deloitte, 'The 2017 Deloitte Millennial Survey. Apprehensive Millennials: Seeking stability and opportunities in an uncertain world' (Deloitte, 2017), www2.deloitte.com/content/dam/Deloitte /global/Documents/About-Deloitte/gx-deloitte-millennial-survey -2017-executive-summary.pdf, accessed 18 May 2021

87 Diversity Project and Qlearsite, 'Return to Work Survey Findings' (Diversity Project, 2020), https://diversityproject.com/resource /return-work-survey-findings, accessed 18 May 2021

88 Timewise, 'Flexible Working: A talent imperative' (Timewise, 2017), https://timewise.co.uk/article/flexible-working-talent-imperative, accessed 18 May 2021

89 N Rathi, 'Why Diversity and Inclusion Are Regulatory Issues', FCA (17 March 2021), www.fca.org.uk/news/speeches/why-diversity -and-inclusion-are-regulatory-issues, accessed 18 May 2021

90 Timewise, 'Timewise Flexible Jobs Index 2020'

91 Practice Business, 'Will Working From Home Remain a Perk Or Become a Right?' (5 June 2020), https://practicebusiness.co.uk/will -working-from-home-remain-a-perk-or-become-a-right, accessed 18 May 2021

92 M Savage, 'Why Finland Leads the World in Flexible Work' (BBC, 8 August 2019), www.bbc.com/worklife/article/20190807-why -finland-leads-the-world-in-flexible-work, accessed 18 May 2021

93 Timewise, 'Timewise Flexible Jobs Index 2020'

94 J Smith, 'Large Majority of People Want to Continue Some Form of Flexible Working', *Insight* (1 September 2020), https:// workplaceinsight.net/large-majority-of-people-want-to-continue -some-form-of-flexible-working, accessed 18 May 2021

95 AM Tuliak and E Stewart, 'Why Our Savings and Investments Project Is More Critical Now Than Ever', Diversity Project Blog (12 May 2020), https://diversityproject.com/2020-05-12/why-our -savings-and-investments-project-more-critical-now-ever, accessed 18 May 2021

96 M Savage, 'How Covid-19 Is Changing Women's Lives' (BBC, 1 July 2020), www.bbc.com/worklife/article/20200630-how-covid-19-is -changing-womens-lives, accessed 18 May 2021

97 Business in the Community, 'Age: Unlock the opportunities of multigeneration teams' (no date), www.bitc.org.uk/age-and -multigeneration-teams, accessed 18 May 2021

98 Diversity Project 2020 Annual Event (no date), https:// diversityproject.com/diversity-project-2020-annual-event

99 HM Treasury and John Glen MP, 'Women in Finance Charter' (HM Treasury, 2016), www.gov.uk/government/publications/women-in -finance-charter, accessed 18 May 2021

100 Business in the Community, 'Race at Work Charter: One year on 2019' (Business in the Community, 2019), www.bitc.org.uk/wp -content/uploads/2019/10/bitc-race-report-raceatworkchartersurvey oneyearoncasestudies-oct2019.pdf, accessed 18 May 2021

101 30% Club, https://30percentclub.org, accessed 16 March 2021
102 Investment 20/20, www.investment2020.org.uk, accessed 16 March 2021
103 ISS, www.issgovernance.com, accessed 16 March 2021
104 A Edgecliffe-Johnson and B Nauman, 'ISS Urges Companies to Disclose Ethnicity of Directors', *Financial Times* (12 July 2020), www.ft.com/content/b45f6a13-c8e6-484b-a75f-bb578178e87f, accessed 18 May 2021
105 Diversity Project, 'Build Back Better' (Diversity Project, 2020), https://diversityproject.com/resource/build-back-better, accessed 18 May 2021
106 Diversity Project, 'Build Back Better'
107 L Morgan Roberts and CL McCluney, 'Working From Home While Black', *Harvard Business Review* (17 June 2020), https://hbr.org/2020/06/working-from-home-while-black, accessed 28 July 2020
108 M Kłopotek, 'The Advantages and Disadvantages of Working Remotely From the Perspective of Young Employees', *Organization & Management Quarterly*, 4/40 (2018), 39–49, http://oamquarterly.polsl.pl/wp-content/uploads/2018/06/03-K%C5%82opotek.pdf, accessed 15 March 2021
109 King's College London, 'Women Doing More Childcare Under Lockdown But Men More Likely to Feel Their Jobs Are Suffering' (25 June 2020), www.kcl.ac.uk/news/women-doing-more-childcare-under-lockdown-but-men-more-likely-to-feel-their-jobs-are-suffering, accessed 15 March 2021
110 ONS, 'Coronavirus (COVID-19) and the Different Effects on Men and Women in the UK, March 2020 to February 2021' (ONS, 2021), www.ons.gov.uk/peoplepopulationandcommunity/healthandsocialcare/conditionsanddiseases/articles/coronaviruscovid19andthedifferenteffectsonmenandwomenintheukmarch2020tofebruary2021/2021-03-10, accessed 15 March 2021
111 Diversity Project, 'A Smart Working Manifesto for Change for the Investment and Saving Industry' (Diversity Project, 2020), https://diversityproject.com/resource/smart-working-manifesto-change-investment-and-saving-industry, accessed 15 March 2021
112 Interview, 15 July 2020
113 Diversity Project, www.diversityprojectcharity.org

Printed in Great Britain
by Amazon